I0824091

In this gorgeous book, Lisa Steele celebrates farm-fresh seasonal produce with stunning, inspiring recipes that compel you to enjoy more fruits and vegetables. This seasonal approach can be a boon to your health—naturally building in a nutritionally balanced variety and making eating well more exciting and flavorful.

—**ELLIE KRIEGER,** registered dietitian, Food Network and PBS show host, and two-time James Beard Award–winning cookbook author

My family and I have been raising our flock of beloved chickens for about ten years now. . . . Even after a decade, I'm still learning, which is why I rely so much on Lisa's sound, relatable advice [to] raise happy, healthy hens and turn their bounty into beautiful meals that rule our breakfast roost. . . . I adore this book, and I know you will too.

—**GENEVIEVE PADALECKI,** actress

As a fellow cookbook author, I appreciate that Lisa brings her signature expertise and warmth to *In Season*. She is the queen of backyard flocks—raising chickens, ducks, and geese for eggs . . . *In Season* is a true reflection of the cook behind it, as Lisa brings her practical, warm, and elegant take on seasonal cooking, and fresh ingredients come to life in the recipes. As someone who values seasonal cooking and thoughtful recipes, I loved every page. This is the kind of cookbook you'll keep on your counter and reach for all year long.

—**TARA BENCH,** author of *Delicious Gatherings* and founder of TaraTeaspoon.com

Lisa Steele! She's done it again.

—**NANCY FULLER,** Food Network personality

As someone who adores cookbooks and beautiful food photography, *In Season* instantly drew me in—the images are a feast for the eyes and a joy for the soul, making you want to head straight to the kitchen. I made two recipes right away; they were easy to follow and absolutely delicious! Lisa Steele's recipes celebrate the bounty of each season, with smart tips for storing fresh produce and preserving herbs that every home cook will appreciate. As a wannabe full-time gardener and homesteader, I find this book not only pleasing to the eye, but deeply inspiring in the kitchen.

—**HILLARY DANNER,** founder of Jenkins Jellies and author of *Sweet Heat: Cooking with Jenkins Jellies*

[The recipes] are simple in the best way, allowing us to focus on and connect with the beauty of ingredients in their natural seasons and see what a difference that makes (in price and flavor!) . . . This book is sure to be a go-to for anyone eager to explore life on the farm, or looking for a simple, yet inspired, weekday meal!

—**ADRIENNE CHEATHAM,** chef, cookbook author, and cohost of *The Chef's Cut* podcast

In Season

125+ Sweet and Savory Recipes Celebrating Simple, Fresh Ingredients

LISA STEELE

PHOTOGRAPHS BY TINA RUPP

In Season

Published by Harper Celebrate, an imprint of HarperCollins Focus LLC.

A Note About Egg Safety: Some of the recipes in this book call for uncooked or partially cooked eggs. Consuming raw or undercooked eggs, such as those in mayonnaise and soft-cooked or poached eggs, may increase your risk of foodborne illness, especially if you have certain medical conditions.

Cover and food photography: Tina Rupp
Lifestyle photography: Betsy Rand
Additional photography: Shutterstock, 174–175
Cover design and art direction: Sabryna Lugge
Interior design: Lori Lynch

ISBN 978-1-4002-5332-6 (HC)
ISBN 978-1-4002-5335-7 (epub)

Printed in Malaysia

26 27 28 29 30 PJM 5 4 3 2 1

Contents

SANDWICHES

VEGETABLES

POACHED EGGS

BAKED AND BROILED EGGS

OMELETS AND QUESADILLAS

DEVILED EGGS

Savory

Sweet

Introduction

In my debut cookbook, *The Fresh Eggs Daily Cookbook*, I focused on lots of basic, classic, foundational egg recipes that I hoped every aspiring (and established!) cook or baker would want to have at their fingertips—dishes like Boston cream pie, lemon meringue pie, crème brûlée, and of course frittatas, quiches, omelets, and the quintessential eggs Benedict. I shared the egg-cooking tips and tricks I've learned over the years and many favorite egg recipes that I find myself going back to over and over—all the dishes that are on regular rotation at our house.

So why another cookbook, you ask? Well, a girl can't live on eggs alone. Although eggs are my signature ingredient, I do cook other things! So this time around, in addition to sharing more fabulous egg recipes, I've also included some sensational soups, salads, sides, and of course desserts to serve alongside your eggs all year long. This food is not only seasonal and simple to make but is also elegant and always delicious. There's something for everyone.

But a bit more about me before we start cooking. In 2009, when we got that first batch of chicks and I dove back into chicken keeping after leaving (*fleeing*) the rural farm life decades before for college, the homestead revival was in full force. I had every intention of becoming a modern-day Laura Ingalls Wilder, making my own goat milk soap and butter, growing all of our food, canning everything under the sun, making bread, stitching quilts, knitting socks, you name it. I was all in.

However, I quickly learned that goats were probably more than I could handle, I hate weeding, and I'm awful at canning. I have killed every sourdough starter I've been given. I'm not even a great gardener, despite having my Master Gardener certification. That said, I can grow garlic like nobody's business—and the same goes for herbs. I did manage to finish one quilt, which we still use on our bed in the winter, and I am a wiz at knitting socks. But as for the rest of it, I had to admit the honest truth that I'm so very grateful for grocery stores. I definitely would not have made it as a pioneer.

So over the years, I have cut back on trying to do everything and have instead focused on the things I do well and enjoy. And I think that's a valuable realization for all of us. You don't have to do *everything* in order to provide your family with a healthier, more sustainable life. Choose your strengths. Do what you love.

For me, the concept of eating seasonally includes lots of eggs because raising chickens is obviously one of my other superpowers. Our diet also includes lots of fresh homegrown herbs (they're a great way to add flavor to a recipe, and they're super nutritious!) and local, seasonal vegetables—asparagus and peas in the spring; berries, melons, and squash in the summer; and root vegetables in the colder months. It may seem cliché, but there's a reason behind these choices.

Eating fruits and vegetables at the height of their freshness not only saves you money (the in-season prices are generally better) but also means taking full advantage of that ingredient's peak natural flavor, nutrition, and texture.

I've organized this cookbook into fairly traditional chapters—soups, salads, sandwiches, etc.—and within each chapter I've arranged the recipes by season. I've color-coded the recipes by season to carry you from spring and summer and through fall and winter. That's not to say you can't cook a summer recipe in the dead of winter, but cooking seasonally just makes sense for so many reasons. The spring and summer recipes tend to be brighter and lighter, while the fall and winter recipes tend to be cozier, comforting, more substantial dishes.

Eating in season means no longer relying on prepared, packaged, or processed ingredients. It means growing and raising what you can, and then making a valiant effort to frequent farmers markets, buy from neighbors who set up roadside stands, and look at labels to see exactly where that box of strawberries in your hand at the grocery store was grown. The more local, the better. On so many levels. And if you can barter, everyone wins. Trade some eggs for a bag of onions. Trade a pint of raspberries for a bushel of apples. Trade what you have for what you need.

In-season cooking for me means satisfying recipes that aren't too complex. Who has time to fuss all day in the kitchen when you have animals to feed and gardens to tend? But that doesn't mean the recipes can't still be sophisticated and elegant and, above all, delicious. It's just a matter of combining interesting flavor profiles using ingredients at the height of their freshness.

I am not great at cooking meat, and while not a vegetarian by any means, I do try to limit the number of animals we eat (of course, we never eat our own chickens, ducks, or geese). But we do eat a lot of fish and shellfish, especially during the off-season, when eggs aren't as plentiful a protein source because—hello!—we live in Maine. It's very important to me to do my part in supporting local farmers and fishers. That's not to say I never use ingredients that can't be found in Maine, but I do try to support the local economy as much as possible.

True to my cooking style, these recipes are partially reflections of my Scandinavian roots, my New England upbringing, and our life here in rural Maine. It's jam-packed with my signature egg recipes, which we do utilize most often as the protein in our diet. But I've also included colorful salads and sides, vibrant vegetables, and other dishes we eat on a regular basis here on our farm to take advantage of the bountiful local ingredients. And of course, I had to include some decadent desserts, because everyone needs to eat dessert—at least every so often.

I hope you will start to think more about eating seasonally, about choosing produce at the height of freshness to get its full benefit in both nutrition and flavor and to lean in to the natural cycles of growth and production. It is my hope that the next time you have extra eggs or a pile of fresh vegetables—whether you grew them yourself or not—and want to do something new and different with them, you'll pick up this cookbook and try one of my recipes. I'm excited to be sharing more of our family favorites that I hope will also become yours.

The Best Ingredients Ensure the Best Results

Because I cook pretty much everything from scratch and don't use tons of ingredients or heavy spices, it's important for each ingredient to be super fresh and delicious. Over the years, I've become partial to certain brands because they perform and taste wonderful time after time.

Baking often calls for ingredients to be at room temperature or softened, and there's a valid reason for that. Cold ingredients can cause the fats in batters to seize up. Eggs whip better if they're not cold. So when a recipe calls for room temperature ingredients, it's important to follow instructions.

Of course, in a perfect world, we would always remember to take the butter, cream cheese, milk, and eggs out of the refrigerator in advance. But the reality, at least for me, is that I often decide to bake on the spur of the moment. Patience is not one of my virtues! So over the years, I've learned a few shortcuts to get my ingredients to room temperature.

Oh, and for reference, "room temperature" is generally considered to be 65 to 70 degrees.

Eggs

If you raise chickens, you'll have glorious fresh eggs most of the year. But even the best layers take breaks from time to time, so if you need to buy eggs, you'll want to look for pasture-raised, organic eggs. They're the gold standard when it comes to commercially farmed eggs. If it matters to you how the hens that laid the eggs you eat were raised and treated, buy pasture-raised. One of the best brands when it comes to hen welfare is Vital Farms.

Substituting eggs: Most recipes call for large chicken eggs. If you're baking and don't have "large" eggs of a consistent size, or you're using a different type of egg—like duck eggs, for example—simply whisk the egg and then weigh out 2 ounces (or 3 tablespoons) of the mixture for each egg in the recipe. If you're making a savory egg recipe, you can use any size egg, and you likely won't even notice the difference.

Warming Eggs

Recipes sometimes call for room temperature eggs. Eggs whip up more easily at room temperature and incorporate better into batters and doughs.

If you have eggs fresh from your own chickens or your local farmers market that haven't been washed yet, you can leave them out on the kitchen counter. I love the convenience of always having room temperature eggs on hand. Plus they're pretty to look at. Unwashed eggs can safely be left out at room temperature for a couple weeks.

Whole Eggs

If you need to warm up eggs and don't feel like waiting around the time it takes to get them to room temperature (which could range from 30 to 60 minutes or more), simply set the eggs in a bowl of warm water for 5 minutes. Drain the water, refill, and repeat as necessary until your eggs have warmed up. Or ladies, just tuck the egg in your bra like my grandmother used to do. (Just be careful not to break it!)

Separated Eggs

Eggs separate more easily when they're cold and the yolks are less likely to break, so if you need to separate your eggs, do that as soon as they come out of the refrigerator. Place the yolks and whites in separate small bowls or ramekins, then set them in a casserole dish or pie plate. Heat a saucepan of water just until bubbles start to form around the edges, then pour the water into the dish or pie plate to come about halfway up the sides of the ramekins. This will warm the eggs more rapidly without cooking them.

Alternatively, you can just let the bowls of yolks and whites slowly come to room temperature while you're measuring and prepping the remaining ingredients.

Butter

I always keep salted and unsalted butter on hand, as I prefer unsalted butter for baking and salted butter for spreading. Either way, I prefer to use European-style butter that contains more butterfat. The butter, whether you're baking with it or smearing it on a bagel, is richer, creamier, and decidedly tastier. Some brands to look for include Plugra, Kerrygold, and local New England brand Cabot Creamery's Extra Creamy Premium Butter. Vitals Farms is another great option; it comes from grass-fed, pasture-raised cows.

Substituting butter: Unsalted butter is the standard in baking because different brands add varying amounts of salt to their salted butter, so it can be difficult to standardize a recipe. However, you can absolutely use salted butter if you're out of unsalted. Just reduce the amount of salt you're adding by about 1/8 teaspoon for every 4 tablespoons of butter in the recipe.

But be aware that salt is hygroscopic, meaning it absorbs liquid from whatever it touches. The salt in salted butter has absorbed and retained liquid from the butter as well as from the surrounding air, which makes salted butter higher in moisture content. This means your mixture might be a bit thin or wet, requiring you to add a bit more flour.

Softening Butter

Depending on how warm your house is, it can take 30 to 60 minutes for a stick of butter straight from the fridge to soften. We keep our thermostat set to 58 degrees in the winter, so I'm always setting my stick of butter on the woodstove in the winter to soften it more quickly. If you don't have a woodstove, you can set the butter on a sunny windowsill to speed up the process. If you have granite countertops, setting a stick of butter there will help speed up the softening process since the granite will transfer its warmth to the butter more quickly than other surfaces—such as a wooden cutting board, the sink, or a plate, for example. (Conversely, granite countertops will also pull heat from your baked goods, cooling them more quickly.)

Other ways to quickly soften butter include cutting it into small cubes or grating it. A hack that's popular online involves filling a glass or mug with hot water, then dumping out the water and quickly setting the glass over your stick of butter. The residual heat from the glass will soften the butter in a few minutes.

You can also use the microwave or a warm oven (or see the previous page for the bra trick).

Whatever you do, take care not to melt the butter if your recipe calls for room temperature butter. Melted butter isn't the same as softened butter and will likely ruin your recipe. How can you tell the difference? Softened, or room temperature, butter will hold its shape, but your thumb will make an imprint in it when you press down. Melted butter, conversely, is self-explanatory. Chilled or frozen butter is also self-explanatory. It's important to use whatever temperature butter your recipe calls for, especially when working with any sort of pastry (pockets of chilled fats help to create flaky crusts).

Salt

For cooking and baking, I use Diamond Crystal Kosher Salt. It's a coarse salt, which I like because it's easy to pinch some between my fingers right from the saltcellar I keep by my stove and crush it into my dish. It also dissolves quickly, so it's great for baking, and it has less sodium than table salt. I always keep finishing salt on hand for sprinkling on top of savory dishes or the tops of my rolls and breads. I love Saltverk Flaky Sea Salt. It's handcrafted in Northern Iceland, and they have some unique blends like Lava Salt and Birch Smoked Salt for fun variety.

Substituting salt: Salt is usually optional in most recipes, but remember that salt doesn't just add "saltiness" to dishes, it also brings out the sweetness and helps to balance the other flavors. But if you are watching your salt, you can reduce the amount of added salt in the recipe, and it will still work.

Milk

I always use whole milk for baking and testing recipes, as I prefer the richness whole milk adds to a dish.

Substituting whole milk: You can usually substitute with 2% milk unless a recipe specifically calls for whole milk. When cooking with very small amounts of milk, you can generally substitute with skim, an alternative milk, or even water. But I recommend sticking to whole or 2% if the recipe calls for larger amounts (or if you're baking).

Buttermilk

Often, the acid in the buttermilk is necessary to activate the baking soda in the recipe, so don't skip the buttermilk.

Substituting buttermilk: If you don't have buttermilk, you can make your own. Add 1 tablespoon of lemon juice or white vinegar to a measuring cup and then fill with regular milk to the 1 cup mark. Whisk, then let it sit for 10 to 15 minutes until it curdles.

Cream

One thing you can always find in my refrigerator is heavy cream. I add it to my coffee, and it's what gets whipped into whipped cream. We are lucky to have a local Maine brand, Oakhurst Dairy, that stocks our store shelves with milk, cream, and sour cream.

Substituting heavy cream and half-and-half: Whole milk, Lactaid, or even 2% milk can sometimes be substituted for half-and-half or heavy cream in recipes, but you will be removing some of the flavor, richness, and fat from the dish. If you don't have any half-and-half, you can make your own by whisking 1/4 cup of heavy cream into 3/4 cup of regular milk. But don't even think about trying to beat anything but heavy cream into whipped cream—it just won't work.

Room Temperature Milk or Cream

Milk or cream often needs to be at room temperature when added to batter so the cold liquid doesn't cause the fats to seize up. A cup of milk will take about 40 minutes to come to room temperature after being measured. To warm the liquid quickly, you can microwave it for 10-second intervals until it reaches room temperature. Otherwise, heat a small saucepan over low heat. When the pan is hot, remove it from the heat and pour in the milk or cream. Stir to warm the liquid evenly.

Cheese

This is a tough one because I love cheese so much. In fact, I have never met a cheese I didn't like—besides that one mango Cheddar I probably wouldn't try again. . . . But in general, you can't go wrong with cheese of any kind. When I need a great Cheddar, I reach for Cabot Creamery. Beyond that, buy whatever cheese you like. However, I do not recommend buying pre-shredded or pre-grated cheese. Always buy blocks and shred or grate at home as needed. Grating it yourself is not only more economical, but it makes the cheese last longer. And that is doubly true for Parmesan (although I once bought the infamous grated Parmesan in the plastic shaker with the green top because I wanted to fill the container with flour for dusting surfaces before rolling out dough).

Substituting cheeses: Different types of cheeses usually can be substituted in these recipes without a problem. Just keep in mind the properties of the cheese. A soft cheese like mascarpone can be replaced with cream cheese or Boursin, or maybe even whipped ricotta. A crumbly cheese like feta or Bleu cheese can stand in for goat cheese. Mozzarella and burrata make good replacements for each other. Melty cheeses like Fontina, Gouda, Gruyère, Havarti, Monterey Jack, or Swiss can all be subbed in for Cheddar. And hard cheeses like Asiago or Pecorino Romano can be used in place of Parmesan. Just remember that each cheese has a different flavor profile, so you will be changing the taste of the recipe—sometimes in a pretty substantial way.

Cream Cheese

When it comes to cream cheese, I recently switched to rich, creamy Cabot Creamery cream cheese. Whether I'm making cheesecake, frosting, or just smearing it on a bagel, I trust that their cream cheese will add just the right consistency and tang to my dish. And it feels good to buy local brands.

Softening Cream Cheese

Cream cheese will take about an hour out of the fridge to reach room temperature to warm up. Placing it on a sunny windowsill or granite countertop will speed up that process.

Mayonnaise

I love to make my own mayonnaise (see my recipe on page 89), but when I need something pre-made, my choice is Primal Kitchen mayonnaise made with avocado oil. I think it tastes the closest to homemade, and the thickness and texture is exactly how I like my mayonnaise. It's not too watery, and it spreads easily.

Oils

In general, you'll be using oil three potential ways in a recipe: in the recipe itself as a binder or to add moisture, in your pan or pot to fry or sauté ingredients, or as a drizzle over meats, vegetables, or salads.

I use La Tourangelle oils in my kitchen. Their neutral oils like avocado and Sun Coco are perfect for frying or baking because of their neutral taste and relatively high smoke points. The last thing you want while you're cooking dinner is your fire alarm going off! Olio Piro is my olive oil of choice. I also like to use coconut oil and peanut oil, depending on the other flavors in the recipe.

For making salad dressings and drizzles, you can use olive or avocado oil, or any oil with a lower smoke point and stronger flavor like toasted sesame or walnut.

Handy Oil Smoke-Point Chart

Different oils have different smoke points, making some more appropriate for high-heat cooking and some better for drizzling. Once an oil starts to smoke, it can begin to burn and break down, so choosing the right oil for your recipe is important.

	Oil Type	Smoke Point (in degrees Fahrenheit)
Low Heat (best for mild sautéing or salad dressings)	Walnut oil	320
	Unrefined coconut oil	325
	Sesame oil	325
	Butter	350
	Extra-virgin olive oil	350
	Lard	375
	Refined coconut oil	375
	Unrefined avocado oil	350–400
Medium Heat (best for sautéing and baking)	Clarified butter (ghee)	375–450
	Vegetable oil	400
	Refined coconut oil	400–450
	Refined sesame oil	410
	Virgin olive oil	420
High Heat (best for stir-frying and frying)	Peanut oil	450
	Refined sunflower oil	450
	Safflower oil	450–500
	Refined avocado oil	480–520

Flour

I use all-purpose flour 99 percent of the time when I cook and bake. I have used whole wheat, almond, pastry, and bread flour at times, but most recipes call for all-purpose, so that's what I always keep on hand. I have never tried gluten-free baking, but I understand there are some gluten-free options out there that work pretty well. You'll have to experiment on your own if that's something that's important to you and your family.

Sugar

White granulated sugar is the universal sweetener, but sometimes you can swap in brown sugar, maple syrup, or honey. Just remember those substitutes will add more liquid to your recipe. Brown sugar is simply regular white sugar blended with molasses; the more molasses in the mix, the darker the sugar. Brown sugar adds a deeper, richer, more earthy flavor to baked goods and also added moisture, so you might need to slightly reduce the amount of liquid in your recipe. Powdered sugar is made by pulverizing white sugar with corn starch, so it's generally not recommended to substitute it for granulated sugar. I don't use artificial sweeteners, but I understand there are some that can be used in baking.

Nuts

Nuts are so nutritious, and I love a handful on top of my salads or in baked goods. I shop at Nuts.com and have never been disappointed with the freshness of their selection (I also buy my candied ginger from them). I store all my nuts in the freezer for a longer shelf life.

Substituting nuts: Usually, different types of nuts can be used in place of what a recipe calls for. The overall taste of the dish will change, so keep that in mind. If nuts are merely being used as a garnish, you can skip them altogether, or use fried onions, sesame seeds, or panko breadcrumbs for a bit of crunch and texture. If nuts are a main component of a dish and you have an allergy, it might make more sense to find another recipe.

Chocolate

I know some cooks and chefs prefer other brands of chocolate, but I swear by Ghirardelli dark, milk, and white chocolate. It's affordable and easy to find either at your local grocery store or online. I use both the bars and the melting wafers. They melt much better than chips. Although I will use the Ghirardelli chips in cookies or muffins when I don't feel like chopping up a whole bar.

Vanilla

I am obsessed with vanilla bean paste. I started using vanilla bean paste years ago and haven't used vanilla extract since. For one thing, paste doesn't have that alcohol taste that extract sometimes has. More importantly, vanilla bean paste has vanilla bean flecks in it. Additionally, the paste doesn't dry out like whole beans do, and it's (slightly) more affordable. Try the paste. I swear by Nielsen-Massey brand. It can be pricey, but I buy the huge 32-ounce bottle, and it lasts forever.

Substituting vanilla: If I haven't sold you on vanilla bean paste, you can safely substitute equal amounts of vanilla extract for the paste.

1 tablespoon vanilla bean paste = 1 tablespoon vanilla extract = 1 vanilla bean

Spices and Herbs

I like to use fresh herbs whenever possible, but when I have to use dried, I use The Spice House brand. I also love their ground spices and spice blends. You might even spy products from The Spice House on *Top Chef*!

Substituting spices, extracts, and herbs: If you have only dried herbs, remember that dried herbs have a more concentrated flavor. One teaspoon of dried herbs is equivalent to one tablespoon of fresh. Herbs all have such distinct flavors, so substituting different herbs in a recipe will completely change the flavor profile—but that's not necessarily a bad thing. So if you don't like cilantro, by all means, use parsley instead!

Some spices can be subbed in for others. If a recipe calls for cardamom, you can use cinnamon. Instead of taco seasoning, I like to use garam masala or curry powder to make a delicious fusion dish. Experiment with spices and spice blends and use what you like.

Food Coloring

I avoid traditional food coloring whenever possible, instead using homemade natural vegetable and food dyes—turmeric for yellow, blueberries or spirulina for blue, yellow onion skins for orange, and beets for pink or red. I keep Color Kitchen Foods' natural dyes on hand for when I don't feel like making my own food coloring. Keep in mind that liquid food coloring will add a bit more moisture to your recipe, while powdered food coloring won't.

Fruits and Vegetables

If a recipe calls for produce ingredients to be chopped or diced, try to make them uniform in size, so they cook in about the same time and you get fairly equal amounts in each mouthful. If a specific size is called for, there's probably a very good reason for that (this goes for meat, as well).

Substituting fruits: Various types of berries can usually be substituted for each other in equal amounts. You might need to adjust the amount of sugar depending on how sweet they are, but if you don't like strawberries, consider raspberries or blueberries—or a combination.

Stone fruits can also be used in place of each other. Apricots, peaches, plums, cherries, etc. generally work the same in recipes. Feel free to swap in your favorite.

Citrus is generally interchangeable, as well. Lemon curd is a classic, but I've also made grapefruit and orange curd. Sugar amounts will need to be adjusted depending on the type of citrus you're using.

Substituting vegetables: Root vegetables can also be switched up with similar results. Try sweet potatoes, parsnips, or even beets in place of white potatoes in hash, roasted on a sheet pan, or in soups and stews. You can even use winter squash like pumpkins or butternut squash in place of your root vegetables.

Summer squash and zucchini are pretty much interchangeable in recipes, but they're not substitutes for winter squash because of their high water content.

Choosing In-Season Produce

By eating various types of produce when they're in season, you are getting them not only at their freshest, most flavorful, and most nutritious but also likely at their best prices and with a greater selection of varieties.

Of course, with the advent of the modern supermarket, it's usually possible to get almost anything any time of the year, but choosing in-season items whenever possible is still a good idea.

Where you live will also dictate when different items tend to be available. Some fruits and vegetables are technically in season for much of the year, but this handy chart should give you a good idea of the seasonality of the most common kinds of produce. It will also help those patronizing local farms, farm stands, or farmers markets to plan their cooking based on what will be available when.

SPRING

Apricots
Asparagus
Avocado
Capers
Carrots
Celery
Cherries
Herbs
Lemons
Lettuce
Limes
Onions
Peas
Radishes
Rhubarb
Scallions
Shallots
Spinach
Strawberries

SUMMER

Beans
Blackberries
Blueberries
Cantaloupe
Chives
Corn
Cucumbers
Eggplant
Figs
Garlic
Honeydew melon
Peaches
Plums
Raspberries
Summer squash
Tomatoes
Watermelon
Zucchini

FALL

Apples
Beets
Brussels sprouts
Butternut squash
Cranberries
Figs
Grapes
Leeks
Mushrooms
Olives
Parsnips
Pears
Pecans
Peppers
Pomegranates
Potatoes
Pumpkins
Sweet potatoes

WINTER

Bananas
Broccoli
Butternut squash
Cabbage
Cauliflower
Kale
Leeks
Oranges
Pineapples
Potatoes
Spinach
Swiss chard
Turnips

How to Best Store Produce

Groceries are expensive and aren't getting any cheaper. So even though I rarely toss out any overripe or spoiled fruits or vegetables (chickens will gladly help out as long as there's no visible mold or rot), having food go bad simply because it wasn't stored properly is hardly optimal.

When trying to figure out which ingredients need to go in the refrigerator and which can be left out at room temperature, you can usually take your cues from the grocery store. If something is in the refrigerator case there, then it should go in the refrigerator at home as well.

On the Countertop

A lot of produce can be left out at room temperature. Much of it is picked before it's ripe, so it will be fine left to ripen on your counter. Once fully ripe, produce will last longer if you refrigerate it. Refrigeration slows down the ripening process.

Some types of fruits and vegetables produce ethylene gas as they ripen, which will cause everything around them to ripen more quickly. These items should not be put in the refrigerator. Leave them out at room temperature, away from other produce.

Apples	Bananas	Onions	Tomatoes

Conversely, if you *want* to ripen your produce quickly, close it up in a brown paper lunch bag with another ethylene-producing food.

Other produce that can be left on the counter include:

Avocados	Honeydew melon	Peaches	Plums
Bell peppers	Mangoes	Pears	Watermelon
Cantaloupe	Nectarines	Pineapple	

Citrus is another type of produce that can be left out on the counter, but it will be good at room temperature for only about a week compared to a month in the refrigerator. I like to leave a small bowl of lemons and limes on the counter to use, then I freeze some (plus oranges) in wedges to use in drinks and cocktails. I freeze some citrus halves to defrost and juice later, and I freeze some whole to zest when I need citrus peel for recipes. Lemons and limes that have been zested can then also be defrosted and juiced. You can also freeze citrus juice in ice cube trays.

Once produce is fully ripe or has been cut, it should be refrigerated if it won't be eaten right away.

In a Cool, Dry Spot

Some types of produce are meant for longer-term storage, so they do best in a cool, dry, well-ventilated spot like a mudroom, pantry, or root cellar.

Acorn squash
Butternut squash
Garlic
Onions
Parsnips
Potatoes
Shallots
Sweet potatoes
Winter squash

In the Refrigerator

Most whole fruits and vegetables should be refrigerated to preserve their quality and extend their life. But if you'll be using them within a day or so, and if you don't have room in the fridge, they will be fine on the counter overnight. They might just dry out or shrivel up a bit. Once you wash or cut into any type of fruit or vegetable, it should always be refrigerated.

Asparagus
Beets
Berries
Broccoli
Brussels sprouts
Cabbage
Carrots
Celery
Cherries
Corn
Cucumbers
Eggplant
Grapes
Leafy greens
Mushrooms
Summer squash
Zucchini

How to Preserve Fresh Herbs

Fresh herbs beat the dried version any day when it comes to flavor and appearance, and there's really no reason you can't have fresh herbs year-round to use in your cooking and baking.

Fresh herbs can be expensive or hard to find in stores at certain times of the year, but most herbs are easy to grow from seed in small pots or containers. You can even regrow cuttings in a glass of water on your kitchen windowsill!

In the spring, garden centers sell potted herbs that you can trim and snip leaves from all summer. I plant a kitchen herb garden on our back deck in an 18 x 24-inch container, and it provides all the herbs I need.

In the cooler months, when herbs won't grow outside, opt for the larger potted herbs at the grocery store instead of buying cut herbs in small plastic containers. Use what you need, then set the pot on the counter. Water it every few days, and your plant will last for weeks and weeks. In the long run, this is way more economical.

I always like to have fresh basil, dill, mint, parsley, rosemary, sage, and tarragon to use in my cooking. Herbs add excellent flavor to both sweet and savory dishes and have a variety of health benefits. Even here in Maine, mint, rosemary, and sage are perennials that come back each spring in my herb garden. In warmer climates, you might be able to grow herbs year-round outside.

Herbs That Are Best Used Fresh

In general, herbs with softer stems that are grassy and herbaceous are better when used fresh. I grow these herbs myself so I always have a fresh supply:

- Basil
- Chives
- Cilantro
- Dill
- Lemongrass
- Parsley
- Tarragon

Herbs That Are Good Fresh or Dried

These herbs, which are usually perennials with woody stems, are equally good fresh or dried:

- Bay
- Lavender
- Marjoram
- Mint
- Oregano
- Rosemary
- Sage
- Thyme

How to Harvest and Store Fresh Herbs

Pruning and trimming your herb plants, whether they are potted or planted outside in a garden, will lead to more growth and a bushier plant with even more leaves. For the best flavor, you should trim the plants on a regular basis, removing the largest leaves before they flower or go to seed, in addition to taking what you need for your cooking or baking. But never trim more than one-third of a plant at one time.

Once you've pruned your plants, or if you purchase fresh herbs at your grocery store or a local farmers market, knowing how to properly store the extras will extend their life. Herbs are too pricey to let them go to waste.

Preserving herbs in water

Basil, cilantro, dill, mint, parsley

Trim the stem ends to get a fresh cut and remove any lower leaves from the bottom inch and a half of each plant. Add an inch of water to a glass and set the stems in the glass. Place the herbs on your kitchen windowsill, or cover loosely with a plastic baggie and place in the refrigerator. Change the water every few days. The plants should last a few weeks, and you can continue pruning the leaves as needed.

Basil and mint will grow roots pretty quickly, and you can plant the cuttings in your herb garden! If you keep them long enough, the other herbs may start rooting as well.

Preserving herbs in a damp paper towel

Oregano, rosemary, tarragon, thyme

These herbs last longest if you roll them in a damp paper towel and put them in a plastic bag in the refrigerator. They should last one or two weeks this way. You can also put the stems in water on the windowsill or in a glass of water in the refrigerator for the longest-lasting storage.

Preserving herbs in a dry paper towel

Chives, sage

These herbs last longest if you roll them in a dry paper towel and put them in a plastic bag in the refrigerator. They should last at least a week this way.

Drying fresh herbs (any type)

You can always pick the leaves from the stems of any of the culinary herbs and dry them for later use. Lay the leaves out in a single layer on paper towels or on a wire cooling rack in a dry spot. You can also tie several stalks together with twine and hang the herbs upside down to dry. Once dried, the leaves can be crumbled or crushed with your fingers and stored in jars in your pantry or cupboard. Depending on the type of herb, its water content, the relative humidity in the air, and the temperature in your house, drying might take a couple days to a week or more.

Freezing fresh herbs (any type)

You can also freeze fresh herbs so they'll be available no matter the time of year. Either freeze the leaves whole or chop the leaves and freeze them in olive oil in an ice cube tray. The thawed cubes can be used later for sautéing fish or vegetables or as dipping oils for bread.

The Right Tools for the Job

Cooking and baking are much more enjoyable with the right tools. Investing in a few good-quality tools will be less expensive in the long run and will make your time in the kitchen more pleasant and successful.

Personally, I'm not a fan of gadgets and appliances that do only one thing. For me to invest my money (and counter or drawer space) in something, it needs to be versatile and do the jobs it's intended for.

Dutch Ovens

I use my Le Creuset Dutch oven for everything from searing roasts and making soup to baking bread and making choux pastry dough. I also use their mini cocottes. Staub also makes nice cocottes, which are great for individual servings of mac 'n' cheese, pot pies, cobblers, or pots de crème. Both companies' products are heavy, solid vessels and are so well made that they're impossible to break or ruin. They heat up evenly and stay hot. These products are definitely an investment but are well worth it if you cook and bake a lot. I have never even owned a slow cooker or Crock-Pot. My Dutch oven does it all.

Frying Pans

I swore off nonstick years ago and switched to mostly stainless steel and cast iron. My Le Creuset enameled cast-iron skillet is my go-to everyday egg pan. I make scrambled and fried eggs in it, and nothing ever sticks. This skillet has a permanent spot on the front left burner of my stove (I'm left-handed, so that's the prime spot).

As far as stainless steel goes, I love the Made In stainless skillets. They perform really well, are nicely balanced, and aren't so heavy that I can't lift them with one hand. I also don't have to worry about scratching them like I do the enameled cast iron.

Omelet and Crepe Pans

Some people claim that it's impossible to make omelets in anything but a nonstick pan, but I disagree. The French brand de Buyer makes beautiful blue carbon steel pans that are the best for making perfect omelets and thin crepes. I also have their mini skillet (it's the perfect size for one egg). The pans are naturally nonstick and are more lightweight than a cast-iron pan, which makes them much easier to tilt for cooking your omelet or crepe evenly.

Pots and Pans

I also love the Made In stainless steel pots and saucepans with lids. I have them in various sizes for heating up soup, leftovers, vegetables, and the like. They're also what I use to make sauces and gravies.

Casserole Dishes

I use Staub and Emile Henry casserole dishes. Both brands offer a wide variety of colors, although I usually just stick with classic white. They're nice, basic dishes that I find myself reaching for over and over.

Food Processor

Cuisinart makes the food processor I use for chopping nuts, making pesto, and more. I've had mine for years, just like my stand mixer. It's a reliable workhorse and is easy to clean, which is a plus.

Blender

I don't use a blender all that often. But I do use my Smeg immersion blender for making mayonnaise and blending soups.

Knives

The two knives I use daily are my chef's knife and my paring knife. Both are Misen knives. The chef's knife is their smaller 6.5-inch version, which I find fits better in my hand than the full-size 8-inch chef's knife. It's nicely balanced and seems to stay sharp forever. I use that knife pretty much every day, for every meal, for anything that needs to be chopped or sliced—vegetables, cuts of meat, etc. I love a paring knife for small jobs like peeling fruits and vegetables or mincing garlic or ginger. I also use it to core fruits, remove strawberry tops—really anything that requires more finesse. I also have a large, serrated knife that I use to slice bread or tomatoes.

Wooden Spatulas and Scrapers

I love Earlywood's line of flat wooden spatulas and scrapers. Handcrafted in Montana, they're great to use with all your cookware since they won't scratch delicate surfaces.

Bowls and More

Farmhouse Pottery in Vermont makes top-quality handmade mixing bowls, pie plates, dishes, pinch bowls, and more in a classic two-tone design. I have a small collection of their line of kitchen accessories. Still, nothing beats a copper bowl for beating egg whites. It can be a bit of an investment, but it's well worth it if you make a lot of meringues or egg white foam.

Range

None of these tools or ingredients would matter without a reliable stovetop and oven. I love my Lacanche range. We installed it when we moved to Maine and the burners run on propane, so an added bonus: I can cook even if we lose electricity. The oven is electric and includes a convection option. It's so beautiful, it makes cooking and baking even more enjoyable, and it turns out perfect dishes time after time.

A Short History of Eggs

It's believed that humans may have been eating eggs for millennia—likely pilfering from the nests of ground-nesting game or jungle birds after observing another animal doing the same. Then, it's speculated, some adventurous soul may have finally dared to climb a tree to pluck eggs from a nest high above the ground. Next came trapping and keeping the birds in captivity for easier egg collecting. The Chinese and Southeast Asians are believed to be the first to domesticate birds for their eggs, while early Egyptian drawings also depict figures carrying baskets of eggs.

Eggs were most likely eaten raw at first, but there are records of ancient Romans eating hard-cooked eggs. Fast-forward a few centuries, and eggs have become so popular and so versatile that it's said they can be prepared a hundred ways (represented by one hundred folds in a chef's toque). Properly cooking an egg is reportedly one way a restaurant chef tests applicants for kitchen jobs.

Brown, white, blue, or speckled eggs are all the same inside. The shell color is dictated solely by the breed of chicken. The yolk color, however, depends on the diet of the hen. Hens fed a more varied diet—including foods that contain the carotenoid pigment xanthophyll—will have darker, more vibrant orange yolks. One sign of eggs from a pasture-raised chicken is a dark orange yolk because the leafy greens and grasses consumed by the chicken are packed with xanthophyll. Brussels sprouts, kale, spinach, carrots, pumpkins, corn, mangoes, and sweet potatoes also contain the carotenoid pigment.

How to Choose Fresh Eggs

Cooking eggs starts with choosing the freshest eggs. If you raise chickens, it's easy enough to keep track of when each egg was laid. (I write the date on the front of the cartons, but you can also write the date in pencil right on the egg!)

If you buy eggs at the grocery store, I have a trick you can use to determine how old the eggs are. On each carton is a three-digit code from 001 to 365 which indicates when the eggs were put into the carton. This is the Julian date, so 001 equals January 1 and 365 equals December 31. You generally want to choose the highest numbered carton because those eggs were laid most recently. Unless it's early in the new year, then a low number is your best bet!

If you have eggs that aren't in a carton for some reason, or if you don't know when they were laid, use this simple trick to tell which eggs are the freshest. Gently drop the egg into a clear glass of water. A very fresh egg will lie flat on the bottom of the glass.

Why is this? As an egg ages, air seeps into it through the pores in the eggshell, making the egg more buoyant. If an egg is a week or two old, one end of it will start to rise from the bottom of the glass. Air will continue to flow into the egg as weeks pass, until the egg is standing straight up. When enough air has entered the egg, it will start to float. Although a floating egg hasn't necessarily gone bad, I generally toss those. Enough time has passed that bacteria—along with the air—might have seeped into the egg and had time to multiply.

Lastly, if you hold an egg up to your ear and shake it, you can tell if it's fresh or not so fresh. The content of an older egg will move around inside the shell because of the air pocket that has been created over time. The insides will sound (and feel) sloshy. A fresh yolk and white will fill the entire shell and won't move around.

In general, an unwashed fresh egg from your chickens or a farmers market will last for at least three or four months in the refrigerator (or two weeks at room temperature). Meanwhile, an egg from the grocery store will be good for four to five weeks after being put in the carton.

How to Cook Eggs

Eggs are so versatile that you have many options for cooking them by themselves. But don't let their simplicity fool you: Eggs can be tricky to master. While these techniques might seem basic, and they are, here are some tips for success and for achieving the best-tasting eggs every time.

Scrambled

Using a whisk or fork, whisk the eggs in a small bowl until frothy and uniform in color. The longer you whisk, the more air you'll incorporate into the eggs and the fluffier they will be. In a small saucepan, heat about 1 tablespoon of oil or butter (or a combination) over low heat. I prefer butter because it gives the eggs a nice flavor. My rule of thumb is between 1 teaspoon to 1 tablespoon of butter per egg depending on how decadent I want my scramble to be.

Once the oil is shimmering or the butter stops foaming, pour the egg mixture into your pan. Using a spatula, move the eggs from the edges to the center to cook them uniformly. For larger curds, move the eggs gently and as little as possible. If you prefer smaller curds, stir or even whisk the eggs in the pan. Remove the eggs from the heat as soon as they set up. The eggs should still be glossy and wet-looking. They'll continue to cook a bit on the plate. If you cook them until they *look* done, they'll actually end up dry and overcooked.

There is some controversy regarding when to salt scrambled eggs. Personally, I find that salting the eggs before I cook them does make them watery, but of course I'm using very fresh eggs with a higher moisture content. For the same reason, I don't generally add any liquid to my eggs either. Salt breaks down the protein bonds in the eggs, so adding it early can result in softer, looser curds. I'm a fan of pretty structured curds, so I prefer to salt my eggs after they're done cooking. However, one benefit of salting the eggs before whisking them is distributing the salt more evenly. You do you! Neither way is wrong. Experiment to see which you prefer.

Why fresh eggs matter for scrambling: As an egg ages, it loses moisture, so older eggs might result in dry scrambled eggs. Fresh eggs generally don't need any liquid added to them, but you can add some milk, cream, or water to moisten dry scrambled eggs. Or you could get creative and add some sour cream, ricotta, or yogurt for bonus flavor and calcium.

Fried

Whether you like your fried eggs sunny-side up, over easy, or over hard, you should start with a hot skillet. You can fry your eggs in oil, butter, bacon grease, or a combination. Butter and bacon grease add nice flavor, while oil has a higher smoke point that can stand the heat better. If you like brown, crispy edges on your eggs, go for the bacon grease or oil. If you prefer softer whites, use all butter and lower heat.

You can even fry your eggs in heavy cream, which is my favorite way to fry them. Instead of using oil or butter, I pour a thin layer of cream into the pan and crack my eggs into it once the cream is bubbling. The cream will separate and caramelize a bit, and your egg whites will be luscious and creamy and delicious. Try adding a few lemon slices to the skillet for a burst of acid and citrus flavor.

Once you've added your fat to the pan (about 1 tablespoon per egg) and it's hot (oil should be shimmering, and butter should be melted and foaming), add the eggs to the pan. Turn the heat down to low and cover the pan, especially if you like your yolks more well-cooked. Let the eggs cook for 2 to 3 minutes. Use a spatula to carefully flip the eggs, remove the pan from the heat, and let the flip side cook using the residual heat from the pan.

Alternatively, if you aren't super confident about flipping the eggs, basting them is an easy way to mimic an over easy egg. You can use a spoon to baste the yolks with the hot fats in the pan while they're cooking.

Why fresh eggs matter for frying: The white of an egg thins out as the egg ages, so a less-than-fresh egg will spread out over your skillet if you try to fry it.

Poached

Poaching intimidates some people, but it really shouldn't. Once you get the technique down, it's rather easy. The perfectly poached egg has a still-runny yolk enveloped in a cohesive blanket of fully cooked whites.

It's important to use cold eggs when poaching. They will hold their shape better than room temperature eggs. I like to crack each egg into a small dish or ramekin first. That way I can check to be sure no pieces of shell have gotten into the dish. (Cracking your egg on a flat surface instead of the corner of the counter or side of the pot helps with that too.) It's also easier to turn the eggs out into the water from a small dish.

Once you have a pot filled with several inches of simmering water, swirl the water into a vortex with the handle of a wooden spoon. Then, one at a time, slowly

slide each egg into the water in the center of the whirlpool. Continue to swirl the water for a few seconds so the whites come together. Set your timer for 2 to 3 minutes.

Once the time is up, use a slotted spoon to remove the eggs from the water. If you press lightly on the yolk, it should yield a bit, but you should feel some pushback. This indicates that the yolk is partially set but still runny. If the yolk is still soft, you can return the egg to the water for a few more seconds. Drain the poached egg on a paper towel–lined plate.

Why fresh eggs matter for poaching: As with frying, the whites of older eggs won't be as cohesive as that of a fresh egg. If your eggs aren't super fresh, you might want to strain your egg whites through a fine-mesh strainer or slotted spoon before poaching them. Otherwise you'll find wispy whites in your poaching water.

Hard-Cooked and Soft-Cooked

Ask ten people the best way to hard-cook an egg, and you'll likely get ten different answers. Trust me, I've tried them all, and the best way to hard-cook eggs is not to boil them but to steam them instead. Into a bamboo steamer or a colander set over a pot of simmering water, add your eggs. Then set your timer: 6 minutes for jammy eggs, 8 to 10 minutes for soft-cooked eggs, or 12 to 14 minutes for hard-cooked eggs. When time is up, use tongs to move the eggs to a bowl of ice water to stop the cooking process. As soon as the eggs are cool enough to handle, you should be able to peel them easily.

Why fresh eggs matter for hard-cooking: As an egg ages and loses moisture, an air sac forms in the empty space in the blunt end of the egg. This means that when you hard-cook older eggs, one end will be concave and misshapen.

Omelets

Omelets can be intimidating, and I'll admit that many times, I've intended to make an omelet but have instead turned it into a scramble! But all it really takes to make an omelet is fresh eggs, the proper tools, good instructions, and some practice. Soon you'll be making omelets with the best cooks.

Over low heat, add butter and a drizzle of olive oil to a shallow skillet with sloped sides. Whisk 2 eggs in a small bowl until they're light and frothy.

Once the butter is melted, add the eggs. Tilt the pan to spread the eggs evenly, cooking them for about 45 to 60 seconds. When they're mostly set, shake the pan or run a rubber spatula around the edge and underneath to loosen the eggs from the pan. Then sprinkle your fillings down the center of the omelet.

Tilt the pan and, using the spatula, fold two sides of the omelet over toward the center.

Another method is to add the filling to one half of the egg, then fold the omelet in half over the filling.

Why fresh eggs matter for omelets: Like scrambled eggs, omelets made with older eggs might be drier. Adding some liquid in the form of milk or water is helpful if you're using older eggs. However, freshness isn't as essential for making omelets as it is for some other methods. The melty cheese and other fillings go a long way toward disguising otherwise blah eggs.

SOUPS

Chilled Pea and Mint Soup

Elegant but so easy to make, this light, refreshing soup is a wonderful way to highlight the flavor of fresh peas from the garden, with just a hint of mint and tarragon to balance out the earthiness. Serve with crackers for a light lunch or at the start of a fancy dinner on a warm late spring evening. You get extra points for growing the peas yourself, but don't worry—if you don't have fresh peas, a bag of frozen peas works too (see the tip at the end of the recipe).

Makes 4 appetizer servings.

2 tablespoons freshly squeezed lime juice (about 1 lime)
2 cups heavy cream
2 tablespoons butter
1 shallot, peeled and minced
3 cups fresh (or frozen) peas, divided
1/4 cup chopped fresh mint leaves, plus 4 whole sprigs for garnish
2 tablespoons chopped fresh tarragon leaves
Kosher salt
Freshly ground black pepper
Crème fraîche or sour cream thinned with a little water, for drizzling

In a small bowl stir the lime juice into the cream. Set the mixture aside to curdle a bit.

Melt the butter in a large, deep saucepan over medium heat. Add the minced shallot and cook, stirring occasionally until translucent and softened, about 2 to 3 minutes.

Add the curdled cream to the pan and bring to a simmer. Add 2 3/4 cups of the peas and stir to cook, about 5 minutes.

Pour the hot mixture into your blender. Add the mint and tarragon. Remove the center insert from the blender cap to allow steam to escape. Drape a kitchen towel over the top of the blender to prevent the mixture from shooting out (or use a food processor or immersion blender). Starting on low speed and gradually increasing the speed, puree the soup until smooth and creamy.

Season with salt and pepper to taste and refrigerate the soup until chilled. When ready to serve, stir to recombine and thin with a bit of water if desired. Pour into soup bowls and garnish with a drizzle of the thinned crème fraîche or sour cream, the remaining 1/4 cup peas, and mint sprigs.

Fresh Tip: To substitute frozen peas for fresh, simply reduce the cooking time to 2 to 3 minutes.

Milk and Egg Breakfast Soup

I need to apologize in advance for not staying true to a traditional Colombian *changua*, which is a common breakfast soup made with milk, eggs, cheese, cilantro, and soaked stale bread. But I loved the idea of a breakfast soup starring eggs, so sticking with the breakfast theme, I swapped a stale bagel for the bread and a mix of parsley and basil for the cilantro. I hope you like it. I also hope you'll look up the classic recipe and give that a try as well! Both are equally delicious.

Makes 2 servings.

1 1/2 cups stale bagel pieces, ripped into bite-size chunks
3/4 cup cubed Gruyère cheese (1/2-inch cubes)
1 1/2 cups whole milk
1 1/2 cups water
2 scallions, chopped, plus more for garnish
2 tablespoons finely chopped fresh basil, plus 4 whole leaves for garnish
2 tablespoons finely chopped fresh parsley, plus 4 whole leaves for garnish
Kosher salt
4 eggs
Freshly ground black pepper

Divide the bagel pieces and Gruyère between two soup bowls.

Add the milk, water, scallions, chopped basil, and chopped parsley to a medium saucepan over medium-high heat. Season with salt and bring to a boil, stirring occasionally. Reduce the heat to a simmer and cook the soup for 3 to 4 more minutes until the liquid is thoroughly heated, continuing to stir so the milk doesn't burn.

Crack each egg and carefully slide it into the liquid. Cook without stirring for 3 minutes, until the whites are set and the yolks are still runny.

Use a ladle or slotted spoon to gently place two eggs into each bowl. Ladle the remaining soup over the eggs, then season with salt and pepper. Garnish with the reserved scallions, basil, and parsley.

To eat, stir the soup to break the egg open and incorporate the melted cheese into the liquid.

Shrimp Ball Egg Noodle Soup with Dill

Not a fan of chicken noodle soup? Me neither! Maybe you'll enjoy this shrimp ball soup with egg noodles instead. It comes together so quickly for a weeknight dinner. My shortcut is using a high-quality prepared seafood stock and store-bought egg noodles for the base, then adding homemade shrimp balls for a simple-to-make soup that's just a little bit different. I can't promise that it will cure a cold, but I can guarantee that you'll feel better right from the first spoonful.

Makes 4 servings.

4 cups seafood stock
1 cup water
1/2 pound raw shrimp, peeled and deveined, divided
2 tablespoons whole milk
1/4 cup panko breadcrumbs
1 egg white, lightly whisked
1 clove garlic, minced
1-inch piece fresh ginger, peeled and grated
2 scallions, white parts minced and green parts sliced
2 tablespoons chopped fresh dill, plus more for garnish
2 1/2 cups uncooked egg noodles (about 4 ounces)
Kosher salt
Freshly ground black pepper

Bring the stock and water to a boil in a large saucepan.

Meanwhile, roughly chop half of the shrimp. Chop the remaining half into a paste (or puree in a food processor). In a large bowl, mix the chopped shrimp, shrimp paste, milk, breadcrumbs, egg white, garlic, ginger, white parts of the scallions, and dill.

Add the egg noodles to the boiling stock. Reduce the heat and simmer for 5 minutes.

Meanwhile, form the shrimp mixture into 12 to 14 tight balls, about 1 inch in diameter. Carefully add the shrimp balls to the soup and simmer for another 5 minutes until the noodles and shrimp balls are fully cooked. The shrimp in the shrimp balls will turn pink when they are done. Season the soup with salt and pepper.

Use a ladle to divide the shrimp balls between four soup bowls. Then ladle the noodles and broth into the bowls. Garnish with the reserved dill and scallion greens.

Finnish Summer Soup

(Kesäkeitto)

This traditional Finnish soup has a thick cream base like a chowder. It is best made in the early summer when you have tender young vegetables like new potatoes, baby carrots, pearl onions, and peas from the garden, yet the air is still cool enough once the sun goes down for a nice warm bowl of soup for dinner. My family lived in Finland for a year when I was in the sixth grade, and our relatives made this soup for us, so creating a recipe similar to the soup I remember eating as a child has been especially meaningful to me. This dish is such a wonderful way to highlight fresh vegetables with minimal fanfare. The simple seasonings let the veggies take center stage.

Makes 4 appetizer servings.

10 new or fingerling potatoes, halved
2 cups whole milk
Kosher salt
10 pearl onions
1 cup baby carrots (about 12)
1 cup fresh green beans, ends trimmed and cut in half (about 12)
1 cup fresh or frozen peas
1 tablespoon all-purpose flour
1 teaspoon granulated sugar
1/2 cup half-and-half or heavy cream
2 tablespoons salted butter
Ground white pepper
2 tablespoons roughly chopped fresh dill, for garnish
1 tablespoon fresh parsley leaves, for garnish

Add the potatoes to a large saucepan with the milk. Season with salt. Bring to a boil, then reduce the heat to low and simmer, stirring occasionally so the milk doesn't scald, until the potatoes are just starting to soften, about 8 minutes. Add the onions and carrots and continue to simmer until the vegetables are just fork-tender, about 5 minutes. Add the green beans and peas.

In a small bowl whisk the flour and sugar into the half-and-half, then add to the saucepan. Cook, stirring occasionally, until the soup thickens a bit and all the vegetables are tender, about 5 more minutes. Remove from the heat and add the butter. Stir until the butter is melted and combined. Season with salt and pepper.

Ladle into bowls and garnish with the dill and parsley.

Chilled Watermelon Soup with Feta and Mint

The pairing of watermelon and feta in a salad has become so popular that I decided to make it a soup! This cold soup is so refreshing on a hot summer day, and I love the play between the sweet watermelon and honey, the salty feta, and the aromatic, herbaceous mint. This soup comes together in mere minutes and can be made up to a day before you plan on serving it.

Makes 4 appetizer servings.

1 mini or 1/2 large watermelon, cut into 1-inch cubes, divided (about 6 cups)
2 ounces feta, crumbled, divided
12 fresh mint leaves, plus whole sprigs for garnish
1 teaspoon lime zest (about 1/2 lime)
2 tablespoons freshly squeezed lime juice (about 1 lime)
1 tablespoon honey
1 teaspoon vanilla bean paste
1-inch piece fresh ginger, peeled and minced
1/4 teaspoon kosher salt

Set aside 4 or 5 cubes of the watermelon per bowl for serving. Add the remaining watermelon to a blender or food processor with 1 ounce of the feta, then the mint leaves, lime zest, lime juice, honey, vanilla bean paste, ginger, and salt.

Blend until smooth. Refrigerate for at least an hour and up to overnight.

When ready to serve, pile the reserved watermelon cubes in bowls, then pour in the soup. Top with the remaining 1 ounce feta, and garnish with fresh mint sprigs.

Fresh Tip: Knock your knuckles on a watermelon to determine if it's ripe. A ripe watermelon should sound hollow and should feel heavy for its size. The underside of a ripe watermelon will be yellow, not white or light green.

Coconut Shrimp Curry Bowl with Jammy Eggs

This noodle bowl is flavored with coconut, ginger, and garlic—perfect flavors for a cool summer evening. Quick and easy, not to mention delicious and filling, it's one of my favorite soups to make on repeat. The jammy egg yolks dripping over the noodles create a velvety sauce that's so rich and satisfying. You can substitute chicken or beef chunks or even pork for the shrimp if you wish. Vegetarian? Just leave out the meat altogether. Either way, you're going to love it when the liquid gold of the egg yolks combines with the subtly spiced broth.

Makes 2 servings.

6 ounces egg noodles
1/2 pound raw shrimp, peeled and deveined
4 teaspoons curry powder
1 teaspoon garlic powder
1 teaspoon ground ginger
1/2 teaspoon kosher salt, plus more to taste
1/4 teaspoon freshly ground black pepper, plus more to taste
2 tablespoons sesame oil, plus more for drizzling
1 (13 1/2-ounce) can unsweetened coconut milk
3 tablespoons butter
4 eggs, soft-cooked and peeled (see page 30 for method)
2 scallions, thinly sliced, for garnish
Sesame seeds, for garnish
Soy sauce, for drizzling

Bring a medium Dutch oven or heavy pot of salted water to a boil. Add the noodles and cook, stirring occasionally, until al dente, about 5 minutes. Drain the noodles and keep warm, reserving 1/4 cup of the cooking water. Dry the pot and set aside.

In a separate bowl toss the shrimp with the curry powder, garlic powder, ginger, salt, and pepper. Heat the sesame oil in the same pot over medium-high. Add the coated shrimp and cook, without stirring, until fragrant and slightly browned on the bottom, about 3 minutes.

Add the coconut milk and reserved pasta water to the pot and bring to a boil. Reduce the heat to medium and cook, stirring occasionally, until the liquid is slightly reduced and the shrimp are fully cooked, 4 to 5 minutes. Stir in the butter and season with salt and pepper to taste.

Divide the noodles between two bowls. Ladle the broth over the noodles. Cut the eggs in half and set 4 halves in each bowl. Garnish with the scallions and sesame seeds, and drizzle some soy sauce and sesame oil over the soup.

Creamy Mushroom Soup with Sherry and Truffle Oil

For years I couldn't stand cream of mushroom soup. But then I realized that it wasn't the soup itself I didn't enjoy—it was thick, gloppy, canned version that wasn't doing it for me. So I set out to create my own recipe. And lo and behold, as is usually the case, the homemade version stands head and shoulders above store-bought. This soup is bold and earthy and creamy—assisted by egg yolks whisked into the soup while it's cooking. And don't skip the sherry. It pairs so nicely with the mushroom flavor. You can use any type of mushroom you prefer (or have on hand), though I personally like a combination. I'll choose a variety from the grocery store, depending on what they have in stock. Button, cremini, or shiitake are all good choices.

Makes 4 servings.

1/4 cup (1/2 stick) butter, divided
1/2 yellow onion, roughly chopped
2 cloves garlic, roughly chopped
14 ounces thinly sliced mushrooms of your choice (about 18 to 20, depending on size)
2 tablespoons all-purpose flour
2 cups chicken broth
1/4 teaspoon freshly grated nutmeg
1/2 teaspoon ground ginger
2 egg yolks
1 cup heavy cream
2 tablespoons sherry
1 teaspoon kosher salt
1/4 teaspoon ground white pepper
Scallions, thinly sliced, for garnish
Truffle oil, for drizzling

Melt 2 tablespoons of the butter in a deep saucepan or Dutch oven over medium-low heat. Add the onion and garlic and cook, stirring occasionally, until slightly softened, about 4 to 5 minutes. Transfer the onion mixture to a bowl.

Add the remaining 2 tablespoons butter to the hot pan and melt. Add the mushrooms. Continue to cook, stirring occasionally, until the mushrooms are lightly browned, about 6 minutes. Remove 3/4 cup of the mushrooms and transfer to a bowl. Then sprinkle the flour into the hot pan and stir to combine.

Add the broth, onion mixture, nutmeg, and ginger to the pan and bring to a boil, then reduce the heat and simmer for about 10 minutes.

Pour the hot soup into your blender. Remove the center insert from the blender cap to allow steam to escape. Drape a kitchen towel over the top of the blender to prevent the soup from shooting out (or use a food processor or immersion blender). Starting on low speed and gradually increasing the speed, puree the soup until smooth and creamy.

In a medium bowl whisk the egg yolks, then whisk in the cream and sherry. To temper the egg mixture and prevent curdling, whisk a few tablespoons of hot soup into the bowl at a time, until you have a few cups of mixture. Pour the warm egg mixture and the remainder of the soup back into the saucepan or Dutch oven. Stir to combine.

Incorporate 1/4 cup of the reserved mushrooms into the soup, saving the rest for garnish. Stir and cook over low heat for another 3 to 4 minutes until warmed through. Season with salt and pepper. Ladle the soup into bowls, then garnish with sliced scallions and the remaining mushrooms, divided between the bowls. Drizzle some truffle oil over the soup and serve warm.

Fresh Tip: You can use fresh or dried mushrooms in this recipe. Just soak the dried mushrooms in warm water for 15 minutes, then drain and pat dry before continuing with the recipe as written.

IN SEASON — FALL

Roasted Butternut Squash Soup with Fried Sage and Garlic Croutons

Peeling and chopping a butternut squash might seem labor-intensive and unnecessary, but roasting those cubes before adding them to the stockpot is what gives this thick, filling soup its full-bodied flavor. Ginger and nutmeg add warmth and coziness to this hearty soup, and sage adds a welcome earthiness.

Makes 6 to 8 servings.

Roasted Butternut Squash Soup

1 (3-pound) butternut squash, peeled and cut into 1-inch cubes
2 tablespoons olive oil
1/8 teaspoon freshly grated nutmeg, plus more for garnish
Kosher salt
Freshly ground black pepper
2 tablespoons butter
2 shallots, chopped
3 cloves garlic, chopped
1-inch piece fresh ginger, peeled and minced
4 cups vegetable broth
12 fresh sage leaves
1/2 cup heavy cream
3 teaspoons maple syrup

Fried Sage

2 tablespoons olive oil
12 fresh sage leaves
Kosher salt

Garlic Croutons

1 tablespoon butter
1/2 cup cubed day-old rustic bread
Kosher salt
1/8 teaspoon garlic powder

For the Soup

Preheat the oven to 425 degrees. Line a rimmed baking sheet with parchment paper. In a large bowl, toss the squash with the olive oil and season with nutmeg, salt, and pepper. Spread the squash cubes on the prepared baking sheet in a single layer. Roast until they start to caramelize and brown, tossing halfway through, about 40 minutes.

Meanwhile, melt the butter in a Dutch oven or large, heavy pot over medium-low heat. Add the shallots and cook, stirring until translucent, about 3 minutes. Add the garlic and ginger and cook for another 30 to 45 seconds, stirring until aromatic. Add the broth, squash, and 12 fresh sage leaves to the pot. Bring to a boil, then reduce the heat and simmer for 2 to 3 minutes until thoroughly heated. Remove from the heat and add the cream and maple syrup, then puree using an immersion blender (or in batches in a regular blender or food processor). Season to taste with salt and pepper.

For the Fried Sage

Heat the olive oil in a medium skillet over medium heat until shimmering. Add the 12 sage leaves—they should immediately sizzle—and cook until crispy, about 30 to 45 seconds. Use tongs or a slotted spoon to transfer the leaves to a paper towel–lined plate to drain. Season with salt.

For the Croutons

Melt the butter in a large skillet over medium heat. Add the bread cubes, sprinkle with salt, and toss to evenly coat with the butter. Cook for a minute or two without stirring until the cubes are browned on the bottom, then stir and cook for a few more minutes. Stir occasionally, until the cubes are browned all over and crispy. Toss with the garlic powder.

To Serve the Soup

Divide the soup between bowls, then top with fried sage leaves and croutons. Grate some additional nutmeg over the top. Pass any extra croutons around the table.

Fresh Tip: Day-old bread makes the best croutons that can hold their own in a soup without getting immediately soggy. But if you don't have any day-old bread, just arrange fresh bread cubes in a single layer on a baking sheet and place in the oven with the squash for a few minutes. This will dry them out and toast them up a bit.

New England Seafood Chowder

New England is known for its clam chowder, but I prefer this seafood chowder. My father-in-law shared his famous fish chowder recipe with me ages ago, and over the years, scallops and shrimp have joined the firm whitefish in the thick, creamy base. This chowder truly captures all the flavors of New England in a bowl and is one of my favorite soups to make in the winter when there's snow on the ground and bread is baking in the oven. It's so hearty and full of flavor. Fresh seafood is best in this recipe, but if you can't find it, you can use frozen (and defrosted) instead.

Serve with slices of warm, thick, crusty bread, and you've got a delicious, satisfying meal.

Makes 6 to 8 servings.

6 slices thick-cut bacon, divided
2 sprigs fresh thyme
2 tablespoons butter
1/2 pound sea scallops (about 10 to 20, depending on size)
1 onion, diced
2 stalks celery, cut into 1/2-inch pieces
2 medium Yukon Gold potatoes, peeled and cut into 1/2-inch cubes
3 tablespoons all-purpose flour
2 cups whole milk
1 cup heavy cream
1 cup fish stock
1 pound whitefish (such as haddock or cod), cut into cubes
1/2 pound medium shrimp, peeled and deveined (about 20 to 25 shrimp)
1/2 teaspoon kosher salt
1/2 teaspoon freshly ground black pepper
1/2 cup fresh or frozen corn
Lemon juice, to taste
Parsley, for garnish

In a large Dutch oven, cook the bacon and thyme over medium-high heat until crispy, about 3 to 4 minutes. Transfer the bacon to a paper towel–lined plate. Crumble the bacon once it has cooled.

Discard the thyme and all but 2 tablespoons of the bacon grease. Add the butter and scallops to the pot and cook the scallops until golden, about 2 minutes per side. Transfer the scallops to a plate.

Add the onion and celery to the pot and cook until soft, about 3 to 4 minutes. Add the potatoes and cook for a minute or two. Reduce the heat to low. Add the flour and stir to combine. Add the milk, cream, and fish stock and cook, whisking, until just simmering. Cook for 15 minutes, stirring occasionally, until slightly thickened.

Season the fish and shrimp with salt and pepper. Add the fish, shrimp, and corn to the pot. Continue to cook over low heat for another 5 to 10 minutes, until the fish and shrimp are cooked through. Add the scallops and most of the bacon, reserving a few tablespoons of bacon for garnish.

Season with salt and pepper. Add lemon juice to taste. Ladle into bowls, and garnish with reserved bacon and parsley.

SALADS

Avocado, Goat Cheese, and Pecan Arugula Salad with Cherry Champagne Vinegar Dressing

This salad is hearty enough on its own to serve as a light dinner in late spring when cherries are in season, but you can top it with some grilled chicken or pork if you want more protein.

Makes 4 servings.

Cherry Champagne Vinegar Dressing

2 tablespoons cherry jam
2 tablespoons champagne vinegar
1/4 cup olive oil
Kosher salt
Freshly ground black pepper

Salad

1 (5-ounce) package arugula
2 avocados, peeled, pitted, and cut into chunks
1 cup cherries, pitted and halved
1/4 cup pecan halves and pieces, toasted
4 ounces goat cheese, crumbled (about 1/2 cup)
Kosher salt
Freshly ground black pepper

For the Dressing

In a small bowl whisk the jam and vinegar together. Then slowly add the oil, whisking until the dressing emulsifies. Season with salt and pepper.

To Assemble the Salad

In a large salad bowl, toss the arugula with enough of the dressing to evenly coat the greens. Arrange on a serving platter or divide between individual plates. Top with the avocado, cherries, pecans, and goat cheese. Season with salt and pepper.

Serve with the remaining dressing on the side.

Smoked Salmon Salad with Lemon and Dill

This tangy smoked salmon salad is on rotation when my dill is ready to harvest in the spring. But is it a salad or a dip? Either way, slather some on a toasted baguette, and you'll get all the flavors of your favorite bagel shop order. I like to leave the salmon in fairly large pieces, so I'm calling it a salad—but feel free to give it a whirl in the food processor to make it more of a dip.

Makes 4 side servings.

1/4 cup mayonnaise (store-bought or homemade using the recipe on page 89)
1 ounce cream cheese, room temperature
2 tablespoons sour cream
2 teaspoons freshly squeezed lemon juice (about 1/2 lemon)
1 tablespoon minced red onion
1 tablespoon chopped fresh dill (or 1 teaspoon dried)
1 tablespoon chopped fresh chives, plus more for garnish
8 ounces sliced smoked salmon, roughly chopped
Freshly ground black pepper
1 baguette, cut into 1/2-inch slices
Olive oil

Whisk the mayonnaise, cream cheese, sour cream, and lemon juice in a medium bowl until smooth. Add the red onion, dill, and chives and stir to combine. Stir in the salmon, season with pepper, and chill until ready to serve.

Brush the baguette slices with olive oil. Heat a large skillet over medium heat, then toast both sides of the bread until golden, 1 to 2 minutes. Garnish the salmon salad with the additional chives and serve alongside the toasted baguette.

Note: I don't add any salt to this dish because the smoked salmon has enough salt on its own. But you can always taste and season as you like.

Strawberry Bacon Salad with Fried Halloumi and Creamy Honey Balsamic Dressing

I'm not a huge fan of leafy green salads. I'm much more apt to eat a salad if it contains some type of fruit and something crunchy besides the lettuce. This salad hits all the right notes and more. The dressing is so creamy and sweet, and the crumbled bacon puts everything over the top. If you don't have any halloumi, you can sub in mini mozzarella balls or even croutons. But do yourself a favor and try frying halloumi. Just be sure to soak the halloumi in water before frying it. Soaking softens the cheese, making it less chewy, while also removing some of the excess salt.

Makes 2 servings.

Creamy Honey Balsamic Dressing

2 tablespoons balsamic vinegar
2 tablespoons mayonnaise (store-bought or homemade using the recipe on page 89)
1 tablespoon honey
Squeeze of lime
1 teaspoon granulated sugar

Salad

4 ounces halloumi cheese
4 slices bacon, roughly chopped
1 romaine lettuce heart, cut or torn into bite-size pieces
8 strawberries, sliced
1/2 cup walnut pieces
Freshly ground black pepper

For the Dressing

In a small bowl whisk the balsamic vinegar, mayonnaise, honey, squeeze of lime, and sugar together until creamy and smooth.

To Assemble the Salad

Slice the halloumi into 8 slices and soak them in a small bowl of cold water.

Heat a medium skillet over medium-high heat. Add the bacon and cook, stirring occasionally, until browned and crispy, about 4 to 5 minutes. Transfer the bacon pieces to a paper towel–lined plate to drain. Wipe out the skillet and place it back on medium heat.

Drain the halloumi slices and pat them dry with a paper towel. Cut into 1/2-inch cubes. In the hot skillet, dry-fry the cheese cubes, turning until golden brown on all sides.

Divide the lettuce between four salad bowls or plates. Add the strawberries, bacon, and walnuts. Top each dish with halloumi, then drizzle with the dressing. Season to taste with pepper.

Salmon Rice Bowls with Cucumber, Avocado, Frizzled Shallots, and Hot Honey Mayo

To be fair, this isn't technically a salad—but there are a lot of veggies in it, and this recipe really wouldn't fit anywhere else! So here it sits. Don't let the number of ingredients deter you. Once you have them on hand, this dish will come together in about 30 minutes and is likely one you'll find yourself making on repeat.

Makes 2 servings.

Garlic Ginger Rice

2 tablespoons sesame oil
1-inch piece fresh ginger, peeled and minced
2 cloves garlic, minced
1 scallion, thinly sliced, whites and greens separated
1 cup sushi rice
Kosher salt

Hot Honey Mayo

1/4 cup mayonnaise (store-bought or homemade using the recipe on page 89)
2 teaspoons honey
2 to 3 tablespoons sriracha hot sauce, depending on how spicy you want it
1/2 teaspoon freshly squeezed lime juice (less than 1/2 lime)
Sesame oil

Frizzled Shallots

1 shallot, thinly sliced into rings
2 tablespoons all-purpose flour
Kosher salt
Freshly ground black pepper
Neutral oil

Salmon Rice Bowls

2 tablespoons plus 1 teaspoon sesame oil, divided
2 tablespoons tamari
8 ounces salmon, skin removed and cut into bite-size chunks
2 teaspoons rice vinegar
2 teaspoons mirin
1 Persian cucumber, quartered lengthwise and thinly sliced
1 tablespoon water
1 tablespoon soy glaze
3 tablespoons mixed black-and-white sesame seeds, plus more for garnish
1 teaspoon firmly packed brown sugar
1 tablespoon neutral oil
1 avocado, peeled, pitted, and thinly sliced

For the Rice

In a medium skillet heat the sesame oil over medium until shimmering. Add the ginger, garlic, and scallion whites and cook, stirring, until they start to soften and become aromatic, about a minute. Remove from the heat.

recipe continues

continued from page 61

In a large pot, combine the rice, a generous pinch of salt, and 1 1/2 cups water. Bring to a boil, then reduce to a simmer, cover, and cook without stirring until the water has been absorbed and the rice is tender, about 15 minutes. Remove from the heat, fluff with a fork, and stir in the ginger, garlic, and scallion mixture.

For the Hot Honey Mayo

In a small bowl whisk the mayonnaise with the honey, sriracha, lime juice, and a few drops of sesame oil. Refrigerate until ready to use.

For the Frizzled Shallots

In a small bowl toss the shallot rings with the flour. Season with salt and pepper. In a Dutch oven over medium-high, heat 1/4 inch of neutral oil, until the oil is shimmering. Add the shallots and cook, tossing with tongs occasionally, until light golden brown, about 3 to 4 minutes. Use the tongs to remove the shallots to a paper towel–lined plate to drain, and lightly season with salt.

For the Salmon

In a shallow dish, combine 1 teaspoon of the sesame oil and the tamari. Then add the salmon, toss to coat, and marinate for 15 minutes. In a small bowl whisk the vinegar and mirin, then add the cucumber. Toss to coat and let sit to marinate.

In a small bowl whisk the water and the soy glaze together. Pour the sesame seeds into a shallow dish.

Sprinkle the brown sugar over the marinated salmon chunks and toss, then press one side of each cube into the sesame seeds. Heat the remaining 2 tablespoons sesame oil in a medium skillet over medium-high heat. Add the salmon, seed side down, and cook until browned and crispy, then turn the cubes with tongs until seared on all sides, about 30 seconds per side. Remove from the heat, add the soy glaze to the skillet, and gently toss the salmon chunks until they are evenly coated.

To Assemble the Rice Bowls

Divide the rice between the bowls, top with the sliced avocado, marinated cucumber, and salmon. Then add a dollop of the spicy mayonnaise and garnish with the frizzled shallots, scallion greens, and additional sesame seeds.

Black and Bleu Berry Salad with Blueberry Balsamic Dressing

This summer salad really highlights the fresh blueberries and blackberries we grow on our property. The crunch of the walnuts is complemented by creamy bleu cheese and a silky blueberry balsamic dressing. I usually use a spring mix, but you can also make this salad with arugula, spinach, or any leafy green. It's a very pretty salad to serve—I just love how the dark purples of the onion, cabbage, and berries pop against the greens. And extra points if you toss some edible flowers on top.

Makes 2 servings.

Blueberry Balsamic Dressing

1/2 cup fresh blueberries
1 tablespoon balsamic vinegar
1 tablespoon honey
2 tablespoons olive oil
1 tablespoon water

Salad

4 ounces mixed greens or spring mix (about 4 cups)
1 cup blueberries
1 cup blackberries
1/2 cup shredded purple cabbage
1/4 cup thinly sliced red onion
1/4 cup walnut halves and pieces, toasted
4 ounces bleu cheese, crumbled (about 1/2 cup)
Freshly ground black pepper
8 fresh basil leaves, for garnish
Edible flowers, for garnish (optional)

For the Dressing

In a small saucepan, heat the blueberries with the vinegar and honey over medium heat. Cook, stirring, until the berries burst and the sauce thickens slightly, about 5 minutes.

Remove the pan from the heat and strain through a fine-mesh strainer, pressing the liquids into a bowl and discarding the solids. Once the liquid cools, slowly whisk in the olive oil and water.

To Assemble the Salad

In a large salad bowl, toss the greens with the blueberries, blackberries, cabbage, red onion, walnuts, and bleu cheese. Season the salad with pepper, drizzle with the dressing, and garnish with the basil leaves and flowers, if using.

Creamy Scandinavian Cucumber Salad with Dill

My mom used to make this traditional Scandinavian cucumber salad in the summer when I was growing up. It highlights fresh cucumbers and dill from the garden. You will want to make this salad on the morning you plan to serve it for lunch or dinner. If it sits for more than a day or so, it can start to get watery, but it does benefit from being chilled for a few hours to let the flavors combine. Although my mom used regular cucumbers, I prefer using smaller Persian or English cucumbers in this salad. You can use either, and you can peel the cucumber and remove the seeds if you wish. I usually do if they're larger and seem tough.

Makes about 4 side servings.

4 Persian or English cucumbers (or 2 regular medium cucumbers), cut in half lengthwise and thinly sliced
1/2 teaspoon kosher salt, plus more to taste
1/2 cup sour cream
2 tablespoons champagne vinegar
1 teaspoon granulated sugar
Freshly ground black pepper
1/4 cup halved and thinly sliced sweet yellow onion
3 tablespoons roughly chopped fresh dill, plus more sprigs for garnish

Put the cucumber slices into a medium bowl or colander and sprinkle with the salt. Toss to combine, then let sit for 1 hour. Drain the liquid, then squeeze the cucumber slices dry with a paper towel or clean kitchen towel.

Whisk the sour cream, vinegar, sugar, and pepper in a medium serving bowl. Stir in the cucumber, onion, and dill. Season to taste with additional salt.

Chill for several hours before serving. Garnish with fresh dill sprigs. Serve as a side or with crackers.

Fresh Tip: Cucumbers turn yellow and taste bitter as they age, so choose firm, dark green cucumbers for your salad to ensure that they are at peak freshness.

Nectarine Panzanella Salad with Poached Eggs and Mint

This light, refreshing salad is one of my favorites in the summer when nectarines are in season, I have loads of fresh mint growing in my herb garden, and I don't really feel like cooking in the heat. This salad is also lovely with peaches or plums. The toasted bread cubes are perfect for sopping up the runny egg yolk.

Makes 2 servings.

1 (7- or 8-inch) baguette or 2 ciabatta rolls cut into 3/4-inch cubes (about 2 cups)
1 tablespoon olive oil, plus more for drizzling
Kosher salt
Freshly ground black pepper
1/4 cup mayonnaise (store-bought or homemade using the recipe on page 89)
1 tablespoon champagne vinegar
2 nectarines, halved, pitted, and diced
2 cups arugula
4 eggs
1/4 cup fresh mint leaves

Preheat the oven to 450 degrees. Pile the bread cubes on a baking sheet. Drizzle with the tablespoon of oil, then toss and season with salt and pepper. Spread the cubes into an even layer, and toast in the oven for 7 to 8 minutes, until lightly browned, stirring halfway through.

Whisk the mayonnaise and vinegar in a large salad bowl. Thin with a bit of water to a drizzling consistency, if necessary. Season with salt and pepper. Toss the nectarines into the bowl with the vinegar and mayonnaise. Add the arugula and mix to coat. Remove the bread cubes from the oven and toss in the bowl until coated with the dressing. Divide the salad among the plates.

Poach the eggs (see page 30 for method). Set 1 egg on top of each salad and garnish with mint leaves. Season with salt and pepper.

Fresh Tip: If you'd rather not use the oven to toast the bread, heat a skillet over medium heat. Toss the bread cubes with the tablespoon of oil, season with salt and pepper, and toast in the skillet, stirring for several minutes until the bread is golden brown and crisp.

Pickled Beet and Goat Cheese Salad with Pine Nuts and Raspberry Balsamic Dressing

My father-in-law used to make the best pickled beets from beets he grew in his garden here in Maine, but sadly he never shared his recipe with me. So jarred beets it is! I'll happily eat this salad as a main meal, sometimes topped with a poached egg or a Panko-Fried Egg Yolk (recipe on page 72), but it's equally at home as a side salad. The pickled beets and honey goat cheese, in particular, provide so much flavor and tang that I find that a simple raspberry balsamic drizzle is all the dressing this salad needs. Can't find honey goat cheese? Regular is fine, but you might want to drizzle some honey on top for a bit more sweetness.

Makes 4 servings.

Raspberry Balsamic Dressing

1/2 cup fresh or frozen raspberries, defrosted
1/2 teaspoon granulated sugar
1 tablespoon balsamic vinegar
1 teaspoon honey, plus more for drizzling
2 tablespoons olive oil

Salad

5 ounces mixed greens (about 4 to 5 cups)
4 ounces honey goat cheese, crumbled
8 ounces whole or sliced pickled beets, diced
2 avocados, peeled, pitted, and diced
1/2 small red onion, diced
1/4 cup pine nuts, toasted
Freshly ground black pepper
4 Panko-Fried Egg Yolks (optional)

For the Dressing

In a small bowl mash the raspberries and sugar. Let sit for 10 to 15 minutes to allow the berries to macerate. Strain the mixture through a fine-mesh strainer into another small bowl, pressing out as much juice as possible. Then whisk in the balsamic vinegar, honey, and olive oil.

To Assemble the Salad

Divide the greens between four plates or bowls. Top with the goat cheese, beets, avocado, onion, and pine nuts.

Drizzle with the dressing and additional honey, if desired. Season with pepper. Top each salad with a Panko-Fried Egg Yolk, if using.

Panko Fried Egg Yolks

Imagine this: a gloriously runny egg yolk enveloped in a crispy crumb coating. These fried egg yolks require a gentle touch to keep them from breaking as you're preparing them, but the effort is well worth it. They're a great way to add protein to any of my salads but are also delicious for snacking. Personally, I love to set one atop a plate of pasta carbonara or cacio e pepe!

Makes 6.

3/4 cup panko breadcrumbs
Kosher salt
Ground white pepper
6 eggs
Neutral oil for frying

In a small bowl season the breadcrumbs with salt and pepper and whisk to combine. Pour half of the mixture into a shallow dish. Carefully separate the eggs, then gently slide each yolk onto the plate of crumbs without breaking the yolk, spacing the yolks out so they are not touching. Discard the whites or save them for another recipe.

Pour the remaining crumbs over the top of the yolks, covering as much of the yolks as possible. Put the plate in the freezer and chill for about 90 minutes or until just starting to firm up.

Heat 1/2 inch of oil in a medium skillet or frying pan on medium-low until shimmering and a pinch of breadcrumbs sizzles when dropped into the oil.

Using a slotted spoon or skimmer, lower one yolk at a time into the hot oil and cook for about 45 seconds until lightly browned, then carefully turn the yolk over and cook the other side for about 20 to 30 seconds. Once golden on both sides, remove from the oil and drain on a paper towel–lined plate. Repeat for all six yolks.

Fresh Tip: Very fresh eggs will work better since the membrane over the yolk on fresh eggs is thicker than on older eggs. This means they will be less likely to break.

Potato Salad with Bacon, Eggs, and Fresh Herbs

Can't decide if you want potato salad or egg salad? You don't have to. This salad includes them both, plus savory bacon, salty capers, frizzled onions, and a mélange of herbs, garlic, and mustard seasonings that makes preparation a breeze.

Makes 6 side servings.

1 red onion, thinly sliced into rings
1 tablespoon all-purpose flour
2 1/2 teaspoons kosher salt, divided
Freshly ground black pepper
4 Yukon Gold or white potatoes, peeled and cut into 1/2-inch cubes
4 slices bacon, divided
1/3 cup mayonnaise (store-bought or homemade using the recipe on page 89)
1/2 cup shredded smoked Gouda
2 teaspoons capers, plus more for garnish
1/8 teaspoon mustard seeds
1/8 teaspoon mustard powder
1/8 teaspoon garlic powder
1/8 teaspoon chopped fresh tarragon, plus more for garnish
1/8 teaspoon chopped fresh dill, plus more for garnish
1/8 teaspoon chopped fresh chives, plus more for garnish
2 eggs, soft-cooked, cooled, and cut into quarters (see page 30 for method)

In a medium bowl toss the onion rings in the flour and season with salt and pepper.

Place the potato cubes in a large pot or Dutch oven. Fill the pot with enough water to cover the potatoes by an inch, then add 2 teaspoons of the salt. Cover and bring to a boil. Reduce the heat and simmer, uncovered, until the potatoes are fork-tender, about 7 to 8 minutes. Drain, rinse under cold water, and place in a large mixing bowl.

Heat the same pot over medium-low heat, then add the bacon and cook until crispy. Remove the bacon from the pot with tongs and drain on a paper towel–lined plate. Return the pot to the heat and increase to medium-high. Add the coated onion rings and cook in the leftover bacon grease, flipping with tongs so the onions cook evenly, until golden brown, about 3 to 4 minutes. Drain the onion rings on another paper towel–lined plate and season with 1/4 teaspoon of the salt.

Crumble the bacon and add half to the bowl of potatoes, reserving the rest for garnish. Add the mayonnaise, Gouda, capers, mustard seeds, mustard powder, garlic powder, tarragon, dill, chives, and the remaining 1/4 teaspoon salt to the bowl and mix until well combined. Scoop the potato salad into a serving dish, then top with the quartered eggs, frizzled onion rings, and the remaining bacon, plus additional capers. Add fresh tarragon, dill, and chives for garnish.

Pear and Feta Salad with Tahini Miso Honey Dressing and Homemade Croutons

This beautiful fall salad combines thin pear slices, walnuts, and salty feta cheese. The tahini miso honey dressing drizzled on top adds just enough sweet creaminess, and the homemade croutons are super quick and easy to brown up on the stovetop—and can be made using any type of roll or bread you have on hand. In fact, it's a great way to use up that last slightly stale hotdog bun! Serve this as a side salad for four, or add some cooked and shredded chicken, steak strips, or other protein and make it dinner for two.

Makes 4 side servings.

Tahini Miso Honey Dressing

4 tablespoons tahini
2 tablespoons white miso
1 teaspoon honey
1/2 teaspoon ground ginger
1 tablespoon olive oil

Homemade Croutons

1 tablespoon olive oil
1 cup cubed day-old or slightly stale bread
Kosher salt
Freshy ground black pepper

Salad

2 tablespoons olive oil, plus more for drizzling
1 teaspoon champagne vinegar
1 head romaine lettuce, torn by hand
1 pear, thinly sliced
4 ounces feta, crumbled (about 1/2 cup)
1 cup walnut pieces and halves
Freshly ground black pepper
Sesame seeds, for garnish

For the Dressing

In a small bowl whisk the tahini, miso, honey, and ginger until the dressing is smooth. Slowly pour in the olive oil, whisking continuously, then add 5 or 6 teaspoons water until the dressing is a thin, drizzling consistency.

For the Croutons

In a medium skillet heat the olive oil over medium heat. Add the bread cubes and season with salt and pepper. Use tongs to toss the cubes and stir until they are evenly browned on all sides.

To Assemble the Salad

In a medium bowl whisk the olive oil and champagne vinegar. Add the lettuce, pear slices, feta, and walnuts, and toss to coat evenly with the oil-and-vinegar dressing. Arrange the greens on salad plates or in bowls.

Divide the croutons between the plates. Drizzle with the tahini dressing, then season with pepper and garnish with the sesame seeds. Pass the remaining dressing and olive oil for drizzling.

Fresh Tip: Although for eating or baking I would typically look for very ripe pears—ones with a faint scent that yield to slight pressure from my fingers—I prefer the pear for this salad to be slightly crunchy and underripe.

Wedge Salad with Bacon Fig Dressing

I love a good steakhouse-style wedge salad made with cool, crisp iceberg lettuce, fresh tomatoes, crunchy bacon, and dotted with crumbles of bleu cheese. It's such an easy salad to put together on the fly. I've tweaked my version for cooler fall evenings by adding a simple but elegant bacon fig dressing that gets spooned over the top.

Makes 4 side servings.

Bacon Fig Dressing

4 slices bacon, chopped
4 tablespoons fig jam
1 teaspoon balsamic vinegar
2 teaspoons olive oil
Freshly ground black pepper

Salad

1 head iceberg lettuce
4 ounces bleu cheese, crumbled (about 1/2 cup)
Freshly ground black pepper
Fresh figs, halved (optional)

For the Dressing

Heat a medium skillet over medium-low heat. Add the bacon and cook, stirring, until browned and crispy and the fat has been rendered. Remove the bacon to a medium bowl, reserving the grease in the pan. Add the jam and balsamic vinegar to the bowl and whisk to combine. Slowly pour in the olive oil, whisking, until emulsified. Add a few teaspoons of the bacon grease and whisk to a drizzling consistency. Season to taste with pepper.

To Assemble the Salad

Remove the core from the head of lettuce, then cut the head into quarters. Place a wedge of lettuce on each of four salad plates. Divide the bleu cheese between the plates. Season each wedge with pepper. Pour the dressing over the wedges and serve with fresh fig halves on the side, if desired.

Sesame Coleslaw

This is my eye-catching purple and green version of coleslaw. I like to use purple cabbage and red onion for bright pops of color alongside romaine (which I sub in for green cabbage), scallions, and parsley, and then add some toasted sesame oil and seeds for a bit of Asian fusion flair. The sesame adds a wonderful subtle nuttiness to the salad. This is such an easy salad to throw together. I find myself making it all the time in the summer to serve alongside hotdogs, sandwiches, or burgers.

Makes 8 side servings.

1/2 cup mayonnaise (store-bought or homemade using the recipe on page 89)
1 teaspoon granulated sugar
Juice from 1 lime
2 teaspoons toasted sesame oil, plus more for drizzling
1 head romaine lettuce, thinly sliced
1/2 head purple cabbage, shredded
1/2 red onion, halved again and thinly sliced
2 scallions, thinly sliced, whites and greens separated
1/4 cup packed fresh parsley leaves
Sesame seeds, toasted, for garnish
Freshly ground black pepper

In a large bowl, whisk the mayonnaise, sugar, and lime juice, then slowly pour in the sesame oil, whisking until smooth and combined. Add 1 teaspoon water, if needed, to thin the dressing a bit.

Add the lettuce, cabbage, onion, and scallion whites to the bowl and toss to evenly coat with the dressing.

Garnish with the scallion greens, parsley, sesame seeds, and pepper. Drizzle with additional sesame oil, if desired. Refrigerate until ready to serve.

Citrus Avocado Salsa Salad

This bright, refreshing salad can be served with crackers or chips like a salsa or spooned over grilled fish or seafood. I'm calling it a "salsa salad" because it's chunkier than a traditional salsa—almost like a fruit salad. It's a great colorful addition to your plate in the dead of winter when everything is snowy and gray, and the creaminess of the avocado plays so nicely with the acidic citrus. It's a great way to highlight and take advantage of winter produce.

Makes 2 side servings.

1 avocado, peeled, pitted, and cut into 1/2-inch chunks
1/2 pink grapefruit, sectioned and cut into 1/2-inch chunks
1 orange, sectioned and cut into 1/2-inch chunks
1/2 red onion, diced
Zest from one lime
1 teaspoon freshly squeezed lime juice
1 tablespoon olive oil
Kosher salt
Freshly ground black pepper
Fresh basil, for garnish (optional)
Crackers or chips for serving (optional)

Mix the avocado, grapefruit, orange, onion, lime zest, lime juice, and olive oil in a medium bowl. Season to taste with salt and pepper, and garnish with the basil, if desired.

Chill until ready to serve with crackers or chips or as a salad or side dish.

SANDWICHES

Fresh Tip: If you don't have buttermilk, you can add 1 tablespoon lemon juice or vinegar to a measuring cup and then fill with whole milk to the 1 cup mark. Let it sit while you measure out your other ingredients. The acidity will curdle the milk, and voilà! Buttermilk.

Buttermilk Cheddar Biscuit Fried Egg Sliders with Honey Sage Browned Butter

These biscuits come together quickly in one bowl and are delicious on their own. With a fried egg and slice of bacon sandwiched between them, they become the ultimate breakfast slider. The drizzle of honey sage browned butter adds next-level flavor.

Makes 8 sliders.

Buttermilk Cheddar Biscuits

1 3/4 cups all-purpose flour, plus more for dusting
1/4 cup cornmeal
2 tablespoons grated Parmesan
2 teaspoons baking powder
1/2 teaspoon baking soda
1/2 teaspoon garlic powder
1/2 teaspoon kosher salt
1/2 cup (1 stick) butter, frozen
1 cup buttermilk
1 teaspoon honey
3/4 cup shredded sharp Cheddar

Honey Sage Browned Butter

1/2 cup (1 stick) salted butter
2 teaspoons honey
16 fresh sage leaves

Sliders

8 slices cooked bacon, broken into halves
8 eggs

For the Biscuits

Preheat the oven to 425 degrees. In a medium mixing bowl, whisk the flour, cornmeal, Parmesan, baking powder, baking soda, garlic powder, and salt. Use a grater to grate the frozen butter into the bowl, then stir to combine. Add the buttermilk and the honey and stir just until the flour is incorporated. Stir in the Cheddar.

The dough will be very wet and sticky. Turn the dough onto a floured surface and roll out to 1/2-inch thick. Cut into 8 circles using a 3 1/2-inch round biscuit or cookie cutter. Wedge the biscuits into a 9-inch square or round baking dish.

Bake the biscuits for 14 or 15 minutes until golden brown on top.

For the Browned Butter

Melt the butter and honey in a small saucepan over low heat. Add the sage leaves and continue to cook until the leaves get crisp and the butter starts to brown. Remove from the heat and transfer the sage to a paper towel–lined plate to drain.

To Assemble the Sliders

Cut the biscuits in half horizontally and brush the inside of each half with some of the browned butter. Lay two pieces of bacon on each biscuit bottom. Fry the eggs and set one on each slider bottom, over the bacon. Finish each with two crispy sage leaves and a biscuit top.

Bacon, Egg, and Cheese Ciabatta Sandwiches with Maple Mayo

This sandwich features creamy, custardy baked eggs plus a fancy-looking bacon lattice that's easier to make than you might think. Baking the eggs slowly keeps them creamy and moist, and overlapping the bacon ensures that you get some crunch in every delicious bite. With bacon, eggs, and cheese sitting atop a ciabatta bun slathered with maple mayo and topped with peppery arugula, this is truly a "square" meal.

Makes 4 sandwiches.

Maple Mayo

1/4 cup mayonnaise (store-bought or homemade using the recipe on page 89)
3 teaspoons maple syrup
Freshly ground black pepper

Sandwiches

Butter for greasing the baking dish
12 slices thick-cut bacon
8 eggs
1/2 cup water
1/4 cup whole milk
1 teaspoon kosher salt, plus more to taste
Freshly ground black pepper
1 ounce arugula (about 1 cup)
Olive oil
4 ciabatta rolls
1 tablespoon butter
4 slices Cheddar or American cheese

For the Maple Mayo

Whisk the mayonnaise and maple syrup in a small bowl until combined. Season to taste with a few generous grinds of pepper.

For the Sandwiches

Preheat the oven to 325 degrees. Grease an 8 x 8-inch square baking dish. Line a rimmed baking sheet with foil.

Cut each strip of bacon in half crosswise so you have two pieces about 4 inches long. Lay three of the half-strips side by side on the prepared baking sheet, then weave three more of the half-strips in a lattice pattern. Repeat with the remaining half-strips of bacon, until you have four lattice squares. Place a second baking sheet on top of the bacon and press it down, so the bacon stays flat as it cooks. Bake until fully cooked, about 40 minutes. Remove the bacon lattices to a paper towel–lined wire rack to cool.

While the bacon is cooking, whisk the eggs in a medium mixing bowl until frothy and no streaks remain. Whisk in the water, milk, salt, and a few grinds of pepper until combined. Pour the eggs into the square baking dish.

recipe continues

continued from page 87

Once the bacon has been in the oven for about 20 minutes, set the baking dish of eggs in the oven and bake until the edges are set, about 18 to 20 minutes (the middle might still be jiggly).

Toss the arugula in a small bowl with a drizzle of olive oil and season with salt and pepper.

When the eggs are finished cooking, remove them from the oven and cool in the pan on a wire rack for a few minutes. Run a knife around the edge of the pan, then cut the baked egg into four even squares.

Cut the rolls in half horizontally and butter the cut sides. Heat a skillet over medium heat and toast the cut and buttered sides of the rolls until golden. Spread the maple mayonnaise on both toasted halves of the "buns," then top each bottom bun with some arugula, an egg square, a slice of cheese, a square of bacon, and a top bun.

Homemade Mayo

Once you start raising chickens, you'll have so many eggs you won't know what to do with them all! One thing I love to make is homemade mayonnaise. This is a classic recipe that is simple to whip up with an immersion blender. Don't have one? A regular blender will work too.

Makes about 1 cup.

- 3 egg yolks
- 1/2 teaspoon coarse stone-ground mustard
- 2 tablespoons freshly squeezed lemon juice (about 1 lemon)
- 1/4 teaspoon kosher salt
- 1 cup neutral oil

In a blender or using an immersion blender, add the egg yolks, mustard, lemon juice, and salt. Pulse a few times to combine. Once combined, add the oil, a tablespoon at a time, pulsing until the oil incorporates into the egg yolks. Once you've added about half the oil, you can start a slow drizzle, continuing to pulse and emulsify the mixture. Continue to pulse until your mayonnaise starts to thicken, lighten in color to a lemon yellow, and is a spreadable consistency. (If it becomes too thick you can add a bit of water to thin it out.)

Use immediately or transfer to an airtight container and refrigerate. Your mayonnaise should last for a week in the refrigerator.

Note: This recipe uses raw eggs. Anyone pregnant, nursing, or with a compromised immune system should take care eating raw or undercooked eggs due to the risk of salmonella. I recommend using only your own cleanest, freshest eggs for this recipe.

Smashed Eggs on Honey Ricotta Toast

I call this my "lazy" egg salad sandwich and look forward to making it each spring when my chickens start laying again. Simply soft-cook a couple of eggs, smear buttered toast with a sweet and savory ricotta whip, then pile the smashed eggs on top. Season with salt and pepper and drizzle with some additional honey, and you've got a delicious breakfast or midday snack.

Makes 2 servings.

2 thin slices sourdough or other rustic bread
2 tablespoons butter, room temperature
1/4 cup ricotta
1/2 teaspoon honey, plus more for drizzling
2 teaspoons grated Romano, divided
Kosher salt
Freshly ground black pepper
3 soft-cooked eggs, kept warm (see page 30 for method)

Spread both sides of the bread with butter and toast in a skillet over medium-high heat until crispy and browned.

In a small bowl whisk the ricotta, honey, and 1 teaspoon of the Romano. Season with salt and pepper. Spread the ricotta whip on one side of each slice of toast.

Roughly smash the soft-cooked eggs with a fork, then season with salt and pepper. Divide between the two slices of toast. Sprinkle with the remaining 1 teaspoon Romano, season with salt and pepper, and drizzle with additional honey.

Peach Caprese Grilled Sandwiches with Fresh Mozzarella and Basil

Subbing fresh, juicy peaches for the tomatoes in a classic caprese sandwich really delivers all the summer vibes. The key is using peaches that are very ripe so the sweet juices mingle with the melty cheese in every bite. A dash of salt on the peaches helps to bring out their sweetness even more. I could happily eat this sandwich every day all summer long.

Makes 2 sandwiches.

2 tablespoons salted butter, room temperature
4 thick slices sourdough or Italian bread
1 (8-ounce) ball fresh mozzarella, sliced into 8 slices
1 medium peach, pitted and cut into 4 thick slices
Kosher salt
Freshly ground black pepper
6 fresh basil leaves
Honey, for drizzling

Butter one side of each of the slices of bread. Heat a skillet over medium-low heat, then put two bread slices, buttered side down, into the skillet. Top each with two slices of mozzarella and two peach slices, then season with salt and pepper. Top each with three basil leaves, and drizzle with the honey. Top each sandwich with the remaining mozzarella slices and the remaining slices of bread, buttered side facing up.

Press down lightly on each sandwich with a spatula, then cover and toast until golden brown, 2 to 3 minutes. Carefully flip the sandwiches and toast on the other side until crisp and golden and the cheese is melty.

Cut the sandwiches in half and serve.

Fresh Tip: A ripe peach should smell sweet and yield slightly to your touch. To ensure that a peach is ripe, choose one with a brown stem. Any green on or around the stem means the peach isn't ripe. To ripen peaches quickly, enclose them in a paper lunch bag overnight. Even better, toss an avocado, apple, or banana in the bag to help the peach ripen even more quickly.

Open-Faced Scandinavian Shrimp and Smoked Salmon Sandwiches

(Smørrebrød)

This traditional Danish breakfast sandwich literally translates to "butter bread." Great for when you have a crowd to feed, my version uses sour cream spread on dark rye or pumpernickel, topped with some classic flavors including dill, shrimp, and smoked salmon. You can substitute plain Greek yogurt for the sour cream if you wish, or even set up a smørrebrød buffet and let your guests assemble their own sandwiches.

Makes 4 sandwiches.

1/4 cup sour cream or plain Greek yogurt
1/2 lemon, zested and juiced, divided
Kosher salt
Freshly ground black pepper
4 thin slices rye or pumpernickel bread, toasted
2 tablespoons olive oil
1/2 small cucumber, thinly sliced
1/2 red onion, thinly sliced
1/2 pound (about 8) large shrimp, cooked and cut in half lengthwise
4 pieces (about 4 ounces) smoked salmon
1 tablespoon capers
2 eggs, hard-cooked (see page 30 for method), peeled, and cut into quarters
Fresh dill, for garnish

In a small bowl mix the sour cream or yogurt and half of the lemon juice. Season with salt and pepper. Spread over one side of each slice of toast.

In a medium bowl whisk the oil, the remaining lemon juice, and lemon zest. Add the cucumber, onion, shrimp, salmon, and capers. Mix well, and let sit for 10 to 15 minutes (as the flavors combine, the red onion will lose some of its sharpness). Season with salt and pepper. Divide among the slices of toast.

Add the quartered eggs to each slice of toast, then drizzle with any oil remaining in the bowl. Garnish with the fresh dill and season with salt and pepper. Serve at room temperature with a knife and fork.

IN SEASON
SUMMER

Double-Decker Salmon Cake Sandwiches with Lemon Dill Mayo

In Maine, we eat a lot of fish. Salmon is a favorite in our house, and I usually just broil or pan-fry it, but when I'm feeling ambitious, I love to make salmon cakes. They don't take much longer to make than filets, and you can serve them with a side or two for dinner—or turn them into sandwiches, as I have here. For sandwiches, don't forget the Lemon Dill Mayo to slather on the bread.

Makes 2 sandwiches.

Lemon Dill Mayo

1/2 cup mayonnaise (store-bought or homemade using the recipe on page 89)
1 teaspoon lemon zest (about 1/3 lemon)
2 teaspoons freshly squeezed lemon juice (about 1/2 lemon)
1 teaspoon finely chopped fresh dill
Kosher salt
Freshly ground black pepper

Salmon Cake Sandwiches

1 pound fresh salmon steak
4 tablespoons olive oil, divided
1 egg
1/4 cup panko breadcrumbs
2 tablespoons mayonnaise
1 clove garlic, minced
Squeeze of lemon juice
2 scallions, thinly sliced, whites and green separated, divided
1/2 teaspoon kosher salt
1/4 teaspoon freshly ground black pepper
1 tablespoon butter
2 sesame seed sandwich buns, sliced open
2 lettuce leaves

For the Mayo

Stir the mayonnaise, lemon zest, lemon juice, and dill together in a small bowl until combined. Season with salt and pepper to taste.

For the Sandwiches

Cut the salmon steak into 1-inch cubes. Heat 2 tablespoons of the olive oil in a large skillet over medium heat. Add the salmon and cook until just cooked through, turning to cook all sides. Remove the cubes to a cutting board or plate and flake the salmon with a fork. Let the salmon cool slightly. Wipe out the skillet.

In a mixing bowl, stir or whisk the egg, breadcrumbs, mayonnaise, garlic, lemon juice, scallion whites and half the greens, salt, and pepper into a thick paste. Stir in the salmon. Divide into four equal portions and flatten them into patties. Refrigerate the patties for at least 20 minutes.

Heat the remaining 2 tablespoons olive oil and the butter in the skillet over medium heat. Cook the patties until golden, turning carefully halfway through, about 2 to 3 minutes on each side. Remove the patties to a plate and add the buns, face down, to the skillet. Cook until toasted. Set the bottom of each bun on a plate. Top with some of the Lemon Dill Mayo, a lettuce leaf, and a salmon patty. Spread more of the mayo on top of the patty. Then top with another patty, more mayo, and the top bun.

Haddock Sandwiches with Cheddar Cheese and Lemon Garlic Aioli

If you grew up in New England, chances are you are familiar with Friendly's and their ubiquitous Fishamajig SuperMelt Sandwiches, which are basically grilled cheese sandwiches with breaded, fried fish and melted American cheese in the middle. My version includes a creamy lemon garlic aioli, buttery garlic sandwich rolls, and a crispy panko coating on the fish. Aah, the childhood memories this one brings back . . .

Makes 2 sandwiches.

Lemon Garlic Aioli

1/4 cup mayonnaise (store-bought or homemade using the recipe on page 89)
1 clove garlic, minced
2 teaspoons freshly squeezed lemon juice (about 1/2 lemon)
2 teaspoons minced fresh parsley
Kosher salt
Freshly ground black pepper

Haddock Sandwiches

2 (4- to 6-ounce) haddock filets
Kosher salt
Freshly ground black pepper
1/4 cup all-purpose flour
1 egg
1/2 cup panko breadcrumbs
2 tablespoons butter, room temperature
2 sandwich rolls, cut open
1 clove garlic, minced
Neutral oil
4 thin slices Cheddar
2 romaine leaves

For the Aioli

Whisk the mayonnaise, garlic, lemon juice, and parsley in a small bowl until combined. Season with salt and pepper to taste.

For the Sandwiches

Pat the fish filets dry and season both sides with salt and pepper. In a shallow bowl or on a plate, whisk the flour with a pinch of salt and pepper. In a second bowl, whisk the egg, and season with salt and pepper. Add the breadcrumbs to a third bowl. Dredge the fish in the flour, then dip into the egg, letting any excess drip back into the bowl. Then press both sides of the fish filets into the panko breadcrumbs.

Butter the rolls, then press the minced garlic into the butter. Heat a medium skillet over medium heat. Place the rolls in the hot skillet, butter side down, and toast until golden, about 2 minutes.

Wipe out the skillet and heat 1/4 inch neutral oil over medium heat. When the oil is heated and shimmering, add the fish and cook until crisp and golden on both sides, about 3 minutes per side. Drain fish on a paper towel–lined plate and top with cheese.

Spread the aioli on the buns, then place a lettuce leaf on the bottom of each bun. Top each with fish and a bun top.

Classic Croque Madame

The croque madame is the quintessential French sandwich, layering ham, a decadent cheesy béchamel sauce, and Dijon mustard between two slices of butter-grilled bread, which are then layered with more sauce and broiled until bubbly. Finally, the sandwich is topped with a fried egg and eaten with a fork and knife. Want to leave off the fried egg? No problem. Simply whisk the egg and dip the sandwich in the beaten egg before pan-grilling it, and you've got a croque monsieur. The "madame" is thought to refer to the fried egg on top looking like a woman's wide-brimmed hat!

Makes 2 sandwiches.

Cheesy Béchamel Sauce

1 tablespoon salted butter
1 tablespoon all-purpose flour
3/4 cup whole milk
3 ounces shredded Gruyère (about 1 cup)
1/4 teaspoon freshly grated nutmeg
Kosher salt
Freshly ground black pepper

Croque Madame Sandwiches

3 tablespoons salted butter, room temperature, divided
4 thick slices country or sandwich bread
4 slices good-quality ham (3 to 4 ounces)
3 ounces (about 1 cup) shredded Gruyère
2 teaspoons Dijon mustard
2 eggs
Dash freshly grated nutmeg
Kosher salt
Freshly ground black pepper

For the Sauce

Melt the butter over medium-low heat. Add the flour and cook, whisking, for about 30 seconds. Add the milk and simmer, whisking, until the mixture thickens, about 3 to 4 minutes. Remove from the heat and stir in the Gruyère until smooth and melty. Season with the nutmeg and salt and pepper to taste.

For the Sandwiches

Preheat the broiler with the rack in the top position. Line a rimmed baking sheet with parchment.

Heat a medium skillet over medium heat. Spread 2 tablespoons of the butter evenly over one side of each slice of bread. Toast the bread in the skillet, butter side down, until each slice is light golden.

Arrange two slices of bread, toasted side down, on the prepared baking sheet. Spread half the cheesy béchamel over the bread slices, then top with the ham and Gruyère. Spread mustard on the untoasted side of the two remaining slices of bread and top the sandwiches with the mustard side down.

Spread the remaining sauce on top of the sandwiches, making sure it completely covers the bread. Broil until the sauce is bubbling and starting to brown in spots and the cheese inside is melted, about 2 to 3 minutes.

Wipe out the skillet. Melt the remaining 1 tablespoon butter in the skillet over medium heat. Crack the eggs into the pan, cover, and cook until the whites are cooked and the yolks are still runny, about 3 minutes. Top each sandwich with a fried egg. Season with additional nutmeg, salt, and pepper to taste. Serve immediately with a knife and fork.

Sriracha Mayo Fried Egg Sandwiches

We make these fried egg sandwiches a little extra by spreading Sriracha Mayo on the buns before toasting them. I'm not generally a fan of super spicy foods, but the sriracha in the mayo provides just the right amount of heat. And those who do want things a bit spicier can drizzle additional sriracha right from the bottle onto their eggs.

Makes 2 sandwiches.

Sriracha Mayo
Makes about 1/2 cup.

1/2 cup mayonnaise (store-bought or homemade using the recipe on page 89)
1 tablespoon sriracha or hot chili sauce
Juice of 1/2 lime
1/2 teaspoon honey
1/8 teaspoon kosher salt

Fried Egg Sandwiches

2 tablespoons butter, divided
2 hamburger buns or sandwich rolls
1 ounce arugula (about 1 cup)
4 eggs
sriracha, for drizzling (optional)

For the Mayo

Whisk the mayonnaise, sriracha, lime juice, honey, and salt in a small bowl. Taste and add more hot sauce if desired. Chill and use within 4 or 5 days.

For the Sandwiches

Melt 1 tablespoon of the butter in a large skillet over medium heat. Split the rolls and slather 1 tablespoon of Sriracha Mayo on each cut side of the bread. Place the cut sides down in the skillet and cook until crispy and browned, about 3 to 4 minutes. Transfer the buns to plates and spread more Sriracha Mayo on the buns, if desired. Top each bottom bun with a handful of arugula.

Melt the remaining 1 tablespoon butter in the skillet. Add the eggs and fry to your liking. Season with salt and pepper and drizzle with sriracha, if desired, depending on how hot you want your sandwich to be.

Stack the eggs on top of the arugula, then top with the top bun.

VEGETABLES

Minted Peas with Goat Cheese and Honey

Fancy Honey-Roasted Carrots with Cardamom, Goat Cheese, and Ginger

Veggie Hash with Fresh Basil

Three-Cheese Tomato Tarts

Eggplant Parmesan Stacks with Basil Marinara

Lemon-Butter-Bath Corn on the Cob with Hot Honey

Maple Bacon–Roasted Brussels Sprouts with Pistachios and Crispy Shallots

Mushrooms Sautéed in Sherry Garlic Butter and Thyme

Vanilla Parsnip Puree

Pub-Style Fries with Garlic Beer Aioli

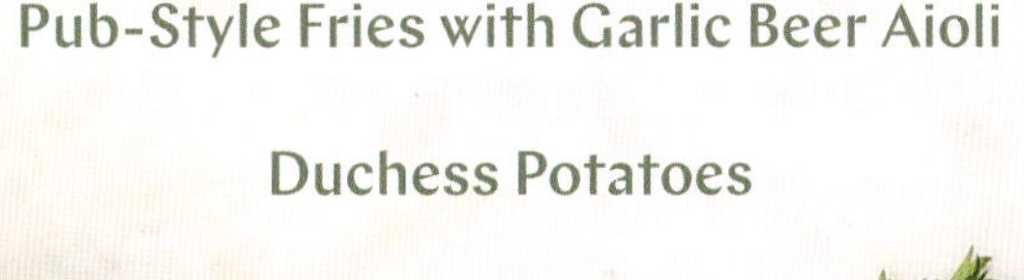

Duchess Potatoes

Minted Peas with Goat Cheese and Honey

You'll want to try this recipe when you have fresh peas from the garden or farmers market. This dish seems so simple and straightforward, which it is, but don't dismiss it for its simplicity. It's a wonderful way to highlight tender spring peas. You can serve it at room temperature or chilled. Fresh peas are best for this recipe, but defrosted frozen peas will also make a lovely dish.

Makes 4 servings.

2 cups fresh peas
1/2 cup packed fresh mint leaves, torn or julienned, plus a few whole leaves for garnish
2 teaspoons honey, plus more for drizzling
1 teaspoon freshly squeezed lime juice (about 1/2 lime)
2 teaspoons olive oil, plus more for drizzling
Kosher salt
Freshly ground black pepper
4 ounces goat cheese, crumbled (about 1 cup)

To blanch the peas and preserve their bright green color, submerge them in boiling water for 1 minute. Use a strainer or slotted spoon to transfer the boiled peas to an ice bath. Leave them in the ice bath for 1 minute, then drain.

In a medium bowl toss the peas with the mint leaves. In a small bowl whisk the honey and lime juice, then slowly drizzle in the olive oil, whisking to combine.

Pour the dressing over the peas, and toss to coat evenly. Season with salt and pepper. Top with the goat cheese and whole mint leaves.

Serve at room temperature or chill until ready to serve. Drizzle with additional honey and olive oil if desired.

Fresh tip: You can also use frozen peas in this recipe. Just defrost them and they're ready to use—no need to blanch!

Fancy Honey-Roasted Carrots with Cardamom, Goat Cheese, and Ginger

Cardamom pairs so nicely with the carrots in this recipe. And roasting the already-sweet carrots in a honey-ginger glaze brings out even more of their sweetness. Orange juice and zest brighten up these veggies, making them the perfect side for your Easter ham or Sunday roast. For this recipe, I prefer to use fancy carrots with tops still attached, purely for aesthetic reasons, but any carrots will work.

Make 4 servings.

2 tablespoons salted butter, melted
2 teaspoons honey, plus more for drizzling
1/2 teaspoon orange zest (about 1/2 medium orange)
1 tablespoon orange juice
1-inch piece fresh ginger, peeled and minced
1 teaspoon ground cardamom
1 pound medium carrots, scrubbed and halved lengthwise (about 8 or 9 carrots)
Kosher salt
Freshly ground black pepper
4 ounces goat cheese, crumbled (about 1 cup)

Preheat the oven to 425 degrees. Line a rimmed baking sheet with parchment paper.

Whisk the butter, honey, orange zest, orange juice, ginger, and cardamom in a medium bowl. Add the carrots and toss to coat evenly. Season with salt and pepper.

Arrange the carrots on the prepared baking sheet in a single layer. Roast for 25 to 30 minutes, turning the carrots occasionally so they roast evenly, until the carrots are fork-tender and starting to brown. Remove them from the oven, top with goat cheese, drizzle with additional honey, and season with salt and pepper.

STAUB
STAUB

Veggie Hash with Fresh Basil

Never underestimate the power of a good sauté to bring out the flavors of vegetables. This isn't your traditional root vegetable hash, but it's definitely not the bag of mixed frozen vegetables your mother used to buy either. This vegetable medley might even change your mind about oft-maligned zucchini. Of course, using fresh veggies is best, but you can substitute frozen vegetables if fresh isn't an option. And rest assured, there's so much going on between the basil and fresh lemon juice, not to mention the peas and corn, that you might not even notice the squash! Be prepared to love this quick and easy summer side. I sometimes like to add a fried egg or two on top to turn this dish into a light summer lunch, but you could also serve the hash with grilled salmon or a grilled chicken breast.

Makes 2 servings.

2 tablespoons olive oil
1 small yellow onion, finely chopped
2 cloves garlic, finely chopped
1 small zucchini, diced into 1/4-inch cubes
1/2 cup corn
1/2 cup peas
Kosher salt
Freshly ground black pepper
1/4 cup packed fresh basil leaves, roughly torn, plus a few whole leaves for garnish
1 tablespoon chopped fresh dill
1 lemon, half zested and juiced, and half cut into wedges
1 tablespoon salted butter

In a large skillet, heat the oil over medium heat until shimmering. Add the onions and garlic and cook, stirring occasionally, until aromatic and softened, about 3 minutes. Add the zucchini, corn, and peas and continue to cook, stirring occasionally, until the vegetables begin to brown in spots, about 6 to 8 minutes.

Remove from the heat, season with salt and pepper, and add the basil, dill, lemon zest, a splash of lemon juice, and the butter. Toss to combine and melt the butter. Garnish with whole basil leaves and lemon wedges.

Three-Cheese Tomato Tarts

I was first introduced to Southern tomato pie by a neighbor when we lived in Virginia. As a tribute to our years there, I was inspired to update the classic by making these individual-size tarts that start with lush, ripe tomatoes sprinkled with salt to coax out some of their juices. Fresh basil and three cheeses top the tomatoes, which are then baked until golden and bubbly.

Makes 8 mini tarts.

Crust

2 cups all-purpose flour, plus more for dusting
1 teaspoon salt
1 teaspoon granulated sugar
1 cup (2 sticks) butter, chilled, cut into cubes
1/4 cup ice water

Filling

4 Roma tomatoes, thinly sliced
Kosher salt
1/2 cup mayonnaise (store-bought or homemade using the recipe on page 89)
1 cup shredded provolone
4 ounces shredded fresh mozzarella (about 1 cup)
1/4 cup grated Parmesan
Freshly ground black pepper
2 tablespoons julienned fresh basil, plus a few whole leaves for garnish

For the Crust

Set out eight 4-inch tart pans.

Combine the flour, salt, sugar, and butter in the bowl of a food processor. Pulse until blended and the butter is mostly incorporated. Add the ice water in a steady stream, pulsing as you pour, until the dough just holds together and forms a ball. Alternatively, make the dough using a pastry blender, then knead.

Flatten the dough into a disc, wrap in plastic, and refrigerate for at least 30 minutes.

Roll out the chilled dough and cut into 5-inch circles, using your tart pans as a guide. Your circles should fit into the bottom and up the sides of the tart pans. Once the pans are lined with dough, prick the bottoms with a fork and chill for 30 more minutes. Preheat the oven to 400 degrees.

Arrange the tart pans on a rimmed baking sheet and bake the crusts for 10 minutes, until light golden. Then remove from the oven and reduce the temperature to 350 degrees.

recipe continues

continued from page 113

For the Filling

While the dough is chilling in the refrigerator for the second time, sprinkle the tomato slices with salt and let them drain in a colander. In a small bowl whisk the mayonnaise, provolone, mozzarella, and Parmesan until combined. Season with pepper.

Once the crusts have been removed from the oven, pat the tomato slices dry with paper towels or a clean kitchen towel. Sprinkle flour over the bottoms of the crusts, then arrange the tomato slices, overlapping them if necessary. Divide the basil between the tart pans. Spoon the cheese mixture over the top and spread to the edges of each tart pan.

Bake the tarts until the tops are bubbly and browned, about 20 minutes. Remove from the oven, let cool for a few minutes, then garnish with basil leaves.

Eggplant Parmesan Stacks with Basil Marinara

These stacks of breaded and fried eggplant, homemade marinara, fresh mozzarella, and basil are so elegant but are super easy to make. They're always on my menu when I have basil, tomatoes, and eggplant growing in the garden. Prepare and salt the eggplant. Then get the marinara going before breading and baking the eggplant. Or if you want to use store-bought marinara to save time, that's perfectly fine too. Just add a few fresh basil leaves as the sauce is warming on the stove, and no one will be the wiser!

Makes 4 stacks.

Basil Marinara

2 tablespoons extra-virgin olive oil
2 cloves garlic, sliced
5 or 6 fresh basil leaves, julienned (about 1 packed tablespoon)
2 tablespoons tomato paste
1 (14-ounce) can crushed tomatoes
1/2 teaspoon granulated sugar
Kosher salt
Freshly ground black pepper

Eggplant Parmesan Stacks

1 medium eggplant, peeled and cut into 8 (1/2-inch) rounds
Kosher salt
2 eggs
1/2 cup panko breadcrumbs
2 tablespoons grated Parmesan
1 teaspoon dried oregano
1 teaspoon dried parsley
Freshly ground black pepper
2 tablespoons all-purpose flour
1/4 cup olive oil
2 tablespoons salted butter
1 (8-ounce) ball fresh mozzarella, cut into 8 slices
Sprig of fresh basil leaves, plus more for garnish

For the Marinara

Heat the oil until shimmering in a medium saucepan over medium-low heat. Add the garlic and basil and cook until the garlic is golden brown and the basil is crispy, about 2 to 3 minutes. Add the tomato paste and cook, stirring, for about 2 minutes, until it turns dark red in color.

recipe continues

continued from page 115

Add the crushed tomatoes and sugar. Stir to combine, then season with salt and pepper, and reduce the heat to a simmer. Continue to cook, stirring occasionally, until the sauce has reduced slightly and has thickened, about 30 minutes.

For the Eggplant

Toss the eggplant slices with 2 teaspoons salt in a colander, then set over the sink. Let sit for 20 minutes. Once the eggplant has sweated, rinse and pat dry with paper towels.

Whisk the eggs in a shallow bowl. In a separate shallow bowl, whisk the breadcrumbs, Parmesan, oregano, and parsley. Season with salt and pepper. Pour the flour into a third shallow bowl and season with salt and pepper.

Heat the olive oil and butter in a skillet over medium heat until the oil is shimmering and the butter is bubbly.

Dredge each eggplant slice in the flour, then the egg wash, then the breadcrumb mixture. Sauté the slices in batches until fork-tender and golden brown on both sides, about 3 minutes per side. Drain on a paper towel–lined plate.

Set four of the eggplant rounds on a rimmed baking sheet, then top each with a spoonful of marinara, a mozzarella slice, and basil leaves, then repeat the layers again, finishing with the mozzarella.

Preheat the broiler and broil the stacks until the cheese is melted and bubbly, about 2 to 3 minutes, but watch closely because broilers can vary. Garnish the stacks with fresh basil leaves and a few grinds of pepper, if desired.

Fresh Tip: Salting the eggplant and letting it "sweat" or "weep" helps to remove some of the excess liquid. The process also softens the eggplant a bit.

Lemon-Butter-Bath Corn on the Cob with Hot Honey

Our neighbor in Virginia grew corn, and he always said, "Start the water boiling, then go pick your corn." He swore that the only way to eat corn was freshly harvested from the garden. But we don't all have that luxury, so I have adapted a Midwestern milk-bath recipe that will result in corn with nice plump kernels that is as sweet as the day it was picked. This is also a great way to serve corn on the cob to a crowd. You won't even need to pass the butter because the corn is basically poached in a butter bath. I still like to serve this corn with Hot Honey Garlic Mayo Dipping Sauce or compound Hot Honey Butter on the side.

Makes 6 servings.

Corn on the Cob

1 cup whole milk
1/2 cup (1 stick) salted butter, cubed
1 teaspoon lemon zest (about 1/3 lemon)
1 tablespoon freshly squeezed lemon juice (about 1/2 lemon)
1 teaspoon granulated sugar
1 teaspoon kosher salt
6 ears of corn, shucked, silk removed, and broken in half
Freshly ground black pepper

Hot Honey Garlic Mayo Dipping Sauce

Makes about 1 1/4 cup.

1 cup mayonnaise (store-bought or homemade using the recipe on page 89)
2 cloves garlic, minced
2 teaspoons honey
2 teaspoons chopped fresh chives
1 teaspoon freshly squeezed lemon juice (less than 1/2 lemon)
Crushed red pepper flakes, to taste
Freshly ground black pepper

Hot Honey Butter

Makes about 1/3 cup.

1/4 cup (1/2 stick) salted butter, room temperature
3 teaspoons honey
2 teaspoons hot sauce
Crushed red pepper flakes

For the Corn

Fill a large pot with 4 cups water. Add the milk, butter, lemon zest, lemon juice, sugar, and salt. Bring to a boil over high heat. Add the corn and reduce the heat to medium. Boil for 8 minutes. Use tongs to remove the corn from the bath, and season with salt and pepper, if desired.

For the Dipping Sauce

Whisk the mayonnaise, garlic, honey, chives, lemon juice, red pepper flakes, and pepper in a small bowl and serve alongside the corn.

For the Hot Honey Butter

Whisk the butter, honey, and hot sauce in a small bowl until smooth. Add red pepper flakes to taste. Serve alongside the corn.

Fresh Tip: Corn on the cob is ready to eat when the husks are a deep, dark green, the silks are browned and dry, and the cob seems heavy for its size.

Maple Bacon–Roasted Brussels Sprouts with Pistachios and Crispy Shallots

This quick and easy recipe will turn even the staunchest naysayer into a fan of Brussels sprouts. These aren't the chewy, watery boiled vegetables your mother used to serve. These Brussels sprouts are roasted in bacon grease at a high temperature to within an inch of their lives to bring out their natural flavors, then tossed with maple syrup and balsamic vinegar for added sweetness. Then they're roasted some more to caramelize everything and are finally sprinkled with chopped pistachios, crispy shallots, and bacon for crunch. The bleu cheese is entirely optional, but I highly recommend it.

Makes 2 servings.

4 slices bacon
1 pound fresh Brussels sprouts, ends trimmed and cut in half
Kosher salt
Freshly ground black pepper
1 tablespoon olive oil
1 shallot, thinly sliced into rings
2 tablespoons maple syrup
2 teaspoons balsamic vinegar
1/4 cup crumbled bleu cheese (optional)
1/4 cup unsalted pistachios, coarsely chopped

Preheat the oven to 425 degrees. Lay the strips of bacon on a rimmed baking sheet and roast until cooked through and crisp, about 14 minutes. Remove the bacon to a paper towel–lined plate to cool, then crumble the strips with your fingers.

Drain any excess bacon grease, leaving just a thin layer on the baking sheet. Add the Brussels sprouts to the baking sheet, season with salt and pepper, and toss them with the bacon grease until uniformly coated. Then arrange the sprouts in a single layer, cut side up. Roast the sprouts on the middle rack for 12 to 15 minutes, until starting to soften and brown around the edges.

While the Brussels sprouts roast, heat the olive oil in a medium skillet over medium-low heat. Add the shallot rings and cook, stirring occasionally, until crispy and evenly browned, about 8 minutes. Season with salt and pepper to taste. Transfer to a paper towel–lined plate.

In a small bowl whisk the maple syrup with the balsamic vinegar and a few grinds of pepper. Remove the Brussels sprouts from the oven and, reserving some syrup for drizzling, use tongs or a spatula to toss them on the pan with the maple syrup mixture. Continue to roast the coated sprouts for another 8 to 10 minutes, until they are crispy and charred in places.

Remove from the oven, toss with the bleu cheese, if using. Season with salt and pepper, and spoon into a serving dish or divide between plates. Drizzle with the reserved maple balsamic glaze, then garnish with the pistachios, shallots, and bacon.

Mushrooms Sautéed in Sherry Garlic Butter and Thyme

A splash of sherry and some fresh thyme bring out the nutty and earthy flavors of mushrooms so beautifully. I prefer to use sherry in my cooking versus sherry cooking wine, which has salt added, but you can use either. Just be sure to taste your dish before adding more salt if you use sherry cooking wine. And resist the urge to stir the mushrooms or move them around too much while they're cooking. This makes them release steam and prevents them from caramelizing as nicely.

Makes 3 to 4 servings.

16 ounces whole cremini or Baby Bella mushrooms (about 2 1/2 cups)
2 tablespoons olive oil
4 sprigs fresh thyme, plus more for garnish
Kosher salt
Freshly ground black pepper
1/4 cup sherry
2 tablespoons butter
2 cloves garlic, minced

Wipe the mushrooms to remove any dirt, then cut into quarters. (If the mushrooms are small, you can leave them whole.)

To a large skillet over medium-high heat, add the oil. Once the oil is shimmering, add the thyme and mushrooms, cut side down, in a single layer and season with salt and pepper. Divide the mushrooms and thyme into two batches if necessary to avoid overcrowding the pan. Cook, without stirring, until the mushrooms start to turn golden brown, about 4 to 5 minutes. Cook for another 3 to 4 minutes, stirring occasionally, until evenly browned.

Remove the mushrooms from the skillet and discard the thyme. Reduce the heat to medium. Deglaze the pan with the sherry, butter, and garlic. Add the mushrooms back to the pan and stir to coat thoroughly. Cook for another minute or two, stirring, until the butter has melted and most of the liquid has evaporated. Remove from the heat, season with salt and pepper, and serve garnished with additional thyme.

Vanilla Parsnip Puree

Parsnips may look like carrots, which makes sense because they're in the carrot family, but they don't taste anything like carrots. They're mildly sweet with an earthy, nutty flavor, which makes them a unique alternative to mashed potatoes. I developed this recipe after taking a cooking class years ago in which we made pureed turnips with vanilla. I thought subbing in parsnips for the turnips might work well—and I was right. I use both a vanilla bean and vanilla bean paste to really amp up the vanilla flavor. Serve this dish at your next holiday gathering, and watch as your guests try to figure out what you did differently with the potatoes this year—while they reach for a second helping!

Makes 4 servings.

1 pound parsnips, washed, peeled, and cut into cubes (about 4 or 5 parsnips)
1 cup whole milk
1/2 cup heavy cream
1 vanilla bean, split in half and the seeds scraped out
2 tablespoons salted butter
1 teaspoon vanilla bean paste
Kosher salt

Add the parsnips, milk, heavy cream, and vanilla bean and seeds to a heavy saucepan, then add water to cover by an inch. Bring to a boil, then reduce the heat and cook at a slow boil until the parsnips are fork-tender, about 12 minutes.

Remove from the heat and use a slotted spoon to transfer the parsnips to the bowl of a food processor. Discard the vanilla bean, but retain 1 cup of the cooking liquid.

Add the butter to the food processor. Then, with the motor running, slowly start adding the cooking liquid. Continue to blend until the puree is silky and smooth. You might not need all the liquid. Add the vanilla bean paste and blend to combine, then season to taste with salt.

Fresh Tip: You can find parsnips in the produce section of many grocery stores in the fall. They're a cold season crop and can also be grown in most cooler climates. Below-freezing temperatures actually improve their flavor. If you can't find parsnips, you could use regular white potatoes or sweet potatoes instead. But do try this recipe with parsnips at least once.

Pub-Style Fries with Garlic Beer Aioli

I'm not particularly a fan of regular French fries, and I don't like ketchup either. But anytime I see sweet potato fries on the menu, I order them—with a side of mayonnaise. I think this stems from living in Virginia, where sweet potatoes appeared on every menu! They've started to make regular appearances at restaurants here in New England in recent years, but in any case, they're really easy to make at home—and the Garlic Beer Aioli dipping sauce is the finishing touch they need. Feel free to use your favorite beer here, both in the batter and the aioli—lagers, pale ales, and craft beers are good choices depending on your flavor preference. I've used both sweet and white potatoes in this recipe, but you can do one or the other. I'm baking mine instead of deep-frying to keep them a bit healthier but still crunchy and delicious.

Makes 2 servings.

Garlic Beer Aioli
Makes about 3/4 cup.

1/2 cup mayonnaise (store-bought or homemade using the recipe on page 89)
2 tablespoons beer of your choice, reserved from the fries recipe
2 cloves garlic, minced
1 tablespoon lemon zest (about 1 lemon)
Kosher salt
Freshly ground black pepper

Pub-Style Fries

1 large sweet potato, scrubbed, peeled, and cut into 1/4-inch sticks
1 russet or Idaho potato, scrubbed, peeled, and cut into 1/4-inch sticks
2 (12-ounce) bottles beer of your choice
2 egg whites
2 tablespoons cornstarch
3 tablespoons olive oil
Kosher salt
Freshly ground black pepper
1 tablespoon chopped fresh parsley, for garnish (optional)

For the Aioli

Whisk the mayonnaise, beer, garlic, and lemon zest in a small bowl. Season to taste with salt and pepper and refrigerate until ready to use.

For the Fries

Preheat the oven to 450 degrees and set a rimmed baking sheet on the middle rack. In a large bowl soak the potato sticks in the beer remaining after making the aioli for 20 to 30 minutes. This process removes some of the starch, resulting in crispier fries. After soaking, remove the potatoes from the bowl and pat dry. In a medium bowl whisk the egg whites until frothy, then add the cornstarch and whisk until no lumps remain. Add the potato sticks to the bowl of batter and use tongs to toss to coat evenly.

Remove the baking sheet from the oven using oven mitts and drizzle the sheet with 2 tablespoons of the olive oil. Use the tongs to remove the potato sticks from the egg-white batter, letting any extra batter drip back into the bowl. Arrange the sticks in a single layer on the baking sheet.

Bake for 10 to 12 minutes, until starting to brown on the bottom. Use a spatula or fish turner to flip the fries, and drizzle them with the remaining 1 tablespoon olive oil. Bake the other three sides for an additional 15 minutes or until browned and crispy all over (nearly 1 hour total). Remove the fries from the oven, season with salt and pepper, garnish with chopped parsley if desired, and serve with Garlic Beer Aioli on the side.

Duchess Potatoes

Dating back to the mid-1700s in France, duchess potatoes are a unique way to elevate the humble potato and, honestly, a really nice change from basic mashed potatoes. Crispy, cheesy, and not difficult to make, these will replace a basic spoonful of mashed potatoes plopped on your guest's plate. Imagine these sitting proudly next to a nice Christmas roast or your Thanksgiving turkey.

Makes about 12 servings.

1 1/4 pounds Yukon Gold potatoes, peeled and cut into 3/4-inch cubes (about 5 or 6 potatoes)
2 teaspoons kosher salt
1/4 cup heavy cream
3 egg yolks
6 tablespoons butter, melted, divided
1/2 cup shredded Gruyère
1/8 teaspoon freshly grated nutmeg
Chopped fresh chives, for garnish
Freshly ground black pepper

Line a baking sheet with parchment paper.

Add the potatoes and salt to a large pot, making sure the potatoes are covered by an inch or two of water. Bring to a boil and cook until fork-tender, about 15 to 20 minutes. Drain the potatoes well, then return them to the pot on the stove. With the burner off, let the potatoes cool slightly in the pot and dry out for 5 to 10 minutes.

To the still-warm potatoes, add the heavy cream, egg yolks, and 2 tablespoons of the butter. Mix with a stand or hand mixer fitted with the whisk attachment until smooth and no lumps remain. Stir in the Gruyère and nutmeg until combined.

Preheat the oven to 400 degrees.

Scoop the potatoes into a pastry bag fitted with a large star tip (I use the Ateco #828), then pipe twelve 2-inch-wide by 2-inch-high mounds of potato onto the prepared baking sheet, about an inch apart.

Drizzle 2 tablespoons of the butter over the tops of the potatoes. Bake for 16 to 18 minutes until the tops are golden brown. Remove from the oven, drizzle with the remaining 2 tablespoons butter, and garnish with chives and black pepper.

LE CREUSET

POACHED EGGS

STAUB
STAUB

Maple Poached Eggs

Here's the perfect recipe for anyone with a sweet tooth. Poaching eggs in maple syrup results in a sticky, sweet egg with a soft creamy white that's great for dipping buttery toast strips. Be sure to use the best quality maple syrup possible. Because maple syrup can get pricey, using your smallest saucepan will allow you to use a relatively small amount of syrup while still covering the egg (I use a 4-inch pan). Also remember that maple syrup gets a lot hotter than water, so watch your egg closely for doneness—optimally you want the yolk to remain liquid—and remove the pan from the heat if it's in danger of bubbling over.

Makes 2 servings.

1/2 cup maple syrup, divided
2 eggs
Freshly ground black pepper
2 slices buttered toast (optional)

Add 1/4 cup of the maple syrup to a small saucepan and bring to a simmer over low heat. Carefully crack an egg into the syrup and cook until the white is set and the yolk is just starting to cook, about 3 minutes.

Use a slotted spoon to carefully remove the egg from the syrup, and set it in a ramekin. Pour the remaining syrup over the egg or serve on the side. Season generously with pepper. Repeat with the remaining syrup and egg.

Serve warm with buttered toast for dipping, if desired. Alternatively, you can serve the eggs over pancakes or waffles.

IN SEASON
SPRING

Poached Eggs with Greek Avgolemono (Egg Lemon) Sauce

This traditional Greek sauce calls for broth or stock—whatever the cook has on hand in the kitchen. My version uses water (although you can absolutely use stock if you have it) and just a light seasoning of salt and pepper at the end. Similar to a hollandaise sauce, you get the satiny smoothness and strong lemon flavor without any butter. The eggs do all the heavy lifting in this frothy, slightly tart sauce, which can be used in place of hollandaise sauce and drizzled over eggs, vegetables, fish, soups, or pasta.

Makes 2 servings.

2 eggs, separated
1 tablespoon all-purpose flour
1/4 cup freshly squeezed lemon juice (about 2 lemons)
4 poached eggs (see page 30 for method)
Kosher salt
Freshly ground white pepper

Bring 1 cup of water to a simmer in a small saucepan. In a small bowl whisk the raw egg yolks with the flour until smooth. Vigorously whisk the raw egg whites and lemon juice in a medium bowl until light and frothy, at least one minute. Whisk the egg yolk mixture into the egg whites.

Add a few spoonfuls of the hot water to the egg mixture, one spoonful at a time, whisking to prevent the eggs from curdling. Then pour the egg mixture into the saucepan of water and cook over low heat, whisking, until the mixture thickens slightly, about 2 minutes. Strain the sauce through a fine-mesh strainer to catch any large bits of eggs. Season to taste with salt and pepper.

Ladle a pool of sauce onto two bowls and top each pool with two poached eggs. Season with salt and pepper. The sauce is best when made just before serving and eaten the same day; it doesn't reheat well.

Poached Egg with Greek Yogurt, Fresh Herb Butter, and Honey

My version of Turkish eggs substitutes in fresh herbs for the traditional chili oil. The mint and parsley mingle with honeyed Greek yogurt under a perfectly poached egg in this twist on a Middle Eastern breakfast classic.

Makes 1 serving.

- 1/2 cup Greek yogurt
- 1/2 teaspoon honey
- Kosher salt
- 1 tablespoon butter
- 1 tablespoon chopped fresh mint
- 1 tablespoon chopped fresh parsley, plus a few whole leaves for garnish
- 1 egg

In a small bowl whisk the yogurt with the honey and a pinch of salt until combined. Allow the mixture to come to room temperature.

In a medium skillet, melt the butter over medium heat. When the butter is bubbling, add the mint and parsley and stir until aromatic, about 30 seconds. Remove from the heat.

Fill a small saucepan with 3 inches of water and bring to a simmer. When bubbles are forming around the edges of the pan, use the handle of a wooden spoon to create a whirlpool in the water, then crack the egg into a small bowl and carefully slide it into the center of the whirlpool. Continue to stir for a few seconds until the egg white starts to set. Cook the egg for 3 minutes, then use a slotted spoon to transfer from the water to a paper towel–lined plate.

Spoon the yogurt into a bowl. Set the egg in the middle, and drizzle with the herb butter. Season with salt and garnish with the reserved parsley leaves.

Poached Eggs over Garlic Ginger Coconut Rice

I love how the warm, runny egg yolk mixes with the creamy coconut rice in this dish. It's a nice, simple, satisfying dish that can be enjoyed any time of the day and served as a side or main course. It's the ultimate summer comfort food: rich, creamy, and delicious with loads of coconut flavor.

Makes 4 servings.

1 tablespoon coconut oil, plus more for drizzling (melted)
2 cloves garlic, finely chopped
One 2-inch piece fresh ginger, peeled and finely chopped
1 1/2 cups uncooked jasmine rice
1 (13.66-ounce) can unsweetened coconut milk
1 teaspoon granulated sugar
2 teaspoons kosher salt, plus more to taste
4 eggs
Freshly ground black pepper
2 tablespoons unsweetened coconut flakes, for garnish
Fresh basil leaves, for garnish

Melt the coconut oil in a Dutch oven or other large heavy pot over medium-high heat. Add the garlic and ginger and stir until aromatic, about 30 seconds. Add the rice and continue stirring until the rice is coated with the oil and starts to toast, about 3 minutes. Stir in the coconut milk, then add 2 cups water. Add the sugar and 2 teaspoons salt. Bring the liquid to a boil, then reduce the heat to a simmer and cook, stirring occasionally, until the rice is done, about 25 minutes.

Meanwhile, poach the eggs (see page 29 for method). Divide the rice between four bowls, then top each with a poached egg. Season with salt and pepper. Drizzle with additional melted coconut oil, then garnish with the coconut flakes and basil.

Butter Beer–Poached Eggs

Why poach eggs in water when you could use beer? This method of poaching results in boozy, silky-smooth eggs with oozy liquid centers. Use any variety of beer you like for this method. An ale or lager will result in tangy eggs, while a pilsner will yield a more mellow flavor. Cheers!

Makes 2 servings.

3 tablespoons butter, divided
1 (12-ounce) can or bottle beer
4 eggs
2 slices buttered toast (optional)

Add 2 tablespoons of the butter and the beer to a medium saucepan over medium-low heat. As soon as the butter is melted and the edges begin to bubble, carefully crack in the eggs, one at a time, swirling the water in a whirlpool around each egg. Cook for about 1 minute, until the whites are just beginning to set.

Use a spoon or ladle to baste the eggs with the beer for several minutes, until the yolks are cooked to your liking and the whites are fully set and no longer translucent. Use a slotted spoon to remove each egg from the poaching liquid.

Continue to reduce the liquid until slightly thickened, then remove from the heat and whisk in the remaining 1 tablespoon butter.

Set the eggs on buttered toast, if desired. Pour the remaining butter beer sauce over the eggs and serve.

Steamed Eggs with Sweet Potato Puree

Those of you familiar with popular restaurant Eggslut in the Grand Central Market in LA might recognize the inspiration behind my version of their signature dish, "The Slut." Since I rarely get out to the West Coast, I couldn't resist adapting their decadent egg dish by making a silky, lightly spiced sweet potato puree topped with heavy cream and a gently coddled egg. You could also use carrot or butternut squash puree if you wish. Of course the buttery toasted baguette for dipping is a must!

Makes 8 servings.

1 medium sweet potato, peeled and cut into 1/2-inch cubes (about 3/4 pound)
1/2 teaspoon kosher salt, plus more to taste
1/4 cup (1/2 stick) butter, cubed
1/4 teaspoon ground ginger
1/4 teaspoon freshly grated nutmeg, plus more for garnish
Freshly ground black pepper
1/2 cup heavy cream, room temperature
8 eggs, room temperature
Baguette, sliced, toasted, and buttered

Set out eight 4-ounce heat-safe mason jars with lids or foil for covering.

Place the sweet potato cubes in a large pot and fill with enough water to cover by 2 inches. Add the salt. Bring the water to a boil and cook the potatoes for 7 to 8 minutes, until fork-tender.

Use a slotted spoon to transfer the potatoes to the bowl of a food processor, retaining the water in the pot. Measure out about 3/4 cup of the cooking water and set aside. Place a wire rack in the bottom of the pot and add water (if needed) to cover the rack by about an inch. Bring the water back to a simmer.

Add the butter, ginger, and nutmeg to the potato cubes, and process until smooth. Add the reserved 3/4 cup cooking water, a little at a time, until the puree is smooth and silky, then season with additional salt and pepper to taste.

Scoop the puree into the mason jars, dividing evenly, and filling to about halfway full. Pour just enough of the cream over the puree to cover with a thin layer, about a tablespoon per jar. Carefully crack an egg on top of the cream in each jar. Set the mason jar lids (but not the rings) on top of the jars—this will allow steam to escape.

Set the jars on the rack in the simmering water (if your pot isn't large enough to hold all the jars at once, cook them in batches). Cook for 12 to 15 minutes or until the egg whites are set but the yolks are still runny. Carefully remove the jars from the water, remove the lids, and garnish with additional nutmeg, salt, and pepper. Serve warm with the buttered baguette slices for dipping.

Norwegian Smoked Salmon Eggs Royale

My first dog ever was a Westie named Oliver (my mother wasn't a "dog" person, so we always had cats growing up). I was newly graduated from college and living on Long Island. He loved bagels and smoked salmon. I created this version of eggs royale on a bagel as an homage to Oliver and my years living and working in New York. I've seen similar recipes called both Norwegian eggs Benedict and eggs royale, so I combined the two. The salty smoked salmon in this recipe works so well with the rich, buttery hollandaise sauce and fresh, herbaceous dill.

Makes 2 servings.

Hollandaise Sauce
Makes about 1 cup.

3 egg yolks
2 tablespoons freshly squeezed lemon juice (about 1 lemon)
1/2 cup (1 stick) butter, cold, cut into 1/2-inch cubes
Kosher salt
Ground white pepper

Smoked Salmon Eggs

1 bagel, cut in half
4 slices smoked salmon (about 4 ounces)
2 eggs
Chopped fresh dill, for garnish
Chopped fresh chives, for garnish

For the Hollandaise

Bring a small pot of water to a boil. In a heatproof glass bowl that will fit over the pot, combine the egg yolks, lemon juice, and 1 tablespoon water. Set the bowl over the pot of boiling water, making sure the boiling water doesn't touch the bottom of the bowl. Whisk the mixture until combined. Slowly add the butter, a few pieces at a time, whisking continuously as the butter melts. Continue to add butter and whisk until the butter is all incorporated.

Cook for another minute or two, continuing to whisk, until the sauce thickens. Season to taste with salt and pepper. Immediately remove from the heat and serve.

For the Eggs

Toast the bagel and place each half on its own plate. Arrange two pieces of salmon on each bagel half.

Poach the eggs in simmering water in a deep saucepan until soft set (see page 29 for method). You really want the yolks to be a bit runny for this recipe, so you're looking at a simmering time of just about 3 minutes. Remove the eggs from the water with a slotted spoon and drain on a paper towel–lined plate, then place an egg on each bagel half. Spoon hollandaise sauce generously over the top, then garnish with fresh dill and chives. Serve immediately.

Eggs Benedict is a classic dish consisting of a poached egg on an English muffin topped with hollandaise sauce. Ham or Canadian bacon is often added as well. Common variations include eggs Florentine, which substitutes spinach for the ham, and this eggs royale variation, which calls for smoked salmon.

Crispy Deep-Fried Poached Eggs

Once you've mastered the perfect poach (see page 29 for method), up your game by deep-frying your poached eggs in a crispy panko crust. These fried eggs are great for topping salads or eggs Benedict or simply for enjoying on a piece of buttered toast.

Makes 4.

5 eggs, divided
1/2 cup all-purpose flour
1 cup panko breadcrumbs
Kosher salt
Freshly ground black pepper
Oil for frying, such as olive, avocado, coconut or peanut

Fill a pot or deep saucepan with a few inches of water and bring to a boil, then turn the heat down to low so the water is just simmering.

One at a time, break four of the eggs into their own small bowls. Next, using the handle of a wooden spoon, swirl the water in the saucepan to create a vortex. Gently slide the eggs, one at a time, into the swirling water. Keep the water swirling around each egg until the whites begin to set.

Cook each egg for 3 minutes, then carefully remove it from the water with a slotted spoon and set on a paper towel–lined plate to drain.

Measure the flour and breadcrumbs into separate shallow dishes and season with salt and pepper. In a small bowl whisk the remaining egg. Arrange the dishes so the flour comes first, then the egg wash, then the breadcrumbs.

Using your hands or the slotted spoon, carefully cover each poached egg with flour, then egg wash, and finally breadcrumbs. Set each breaded egg on a wire rack.

Heat 3 inches of oil in a deep, heavy pot to 375 degrees. Carefully add the eggs to the oil and cook for 45 to 50 seconds until the coating is crisp and golden brown on both sides.

Remove to the wire rack to drain. Serve warm.

BAKED AND BROILED EGGS

Quiche with Fresh Herbs and Cheese

Finnish Oven Pancake (Pannukakku) with Ricotta Honey Whip, Peas, and Asparagus

Creamy Baked Eggs with Parmesan, Black Olives, and Fresh Herbs

Asparagus, Cheddar, and Scallion Frittata

Bacon, Egg, and Cheese French Toast Bake

One-Pan Baked Creamy Eggs on Toast (Oeufs au Plat Bressanne)

Finnish Oven Pancakes (Pannukakku) with Caramelized Onions, Walnuts, and Fontina

Crunchy Baked Vanilla Bourbon French Toast Sticks

Egg and Mushroom Tart

Monte Cristo Breakfast Bake

Mini Charcuterie Stratas

Quiche with Fresh Herbs and Cheese

I always plant herbs in a small container on our back deck so I have them to cook with all summer long. This is one of my favorite recipes to make once the herbs are ready to be harvested and we have plenty of fresh eggs from our chickens. I always make my own pie crust, but if you aren't that ambitious and don't have an herb garden—or chickens—store-bought will work just fine, as Ina Garten likes to remind us. But do yourself a favor and find a local farmers' market to source your ingredients for this one, if you can. Remember, fresh is best.

Makes 1 quiche.

Homemade Pie Crust

1 1/4 cups all-purpose flour
1/2 teaspoon kosher salt
1/2 cup (1 stick) butter, chilled, cut into cubes
1/4 cup ice water

Quiche Filling

3 ounces fresh mozzarella, cubed (about 1/2 cup)
3 ounces cream cheese, cubed
2 ounces feta, crumbled (about 1/4 cup)
2 cloves garlic, chopped
2 tablespoons chopped fresh dill
2 tablespoons chopped fresh basil
2 tablespoons chopped fresh parsley
2 tablespoons chopped fresh chives
5 eggs
3/4 cup half-and-half
Kosher salt
Freshly ground black pepper
2 scallions, thinly sliced

For the Crust

In the bowl of a food processor, combine the flour and salt. Add the butter and pulse about ten times. With the motor running, add the ice water in a slow stream and process just until the dough holds together. (Alternatively, cut the butter into the flour with a pastry cutter, then slowly add the water to the dough and knead.) Flatten the dough into a disc and wrap in plastic wrap. Chill for an hour.

Preheat the oven to 375 degrees. Roll out your pie crust dough and fit into a 9-inch pie plate. Prick with a fork, then cover the crust with foil and fill the dish with pie weights. Refrigerate the crust while the oven heats.

Bake the crust until just starting to turn golden, about 20 minutes. (The crust will finish baking once you add the filling.) Remove from the oven, and remove the weights and foil. Reduce the oven temperature to 325 degrees.

For the Filling

Dot the mozzarella, cream cheese cubes, feta, garlic, dill, basil, parsley, and chives over the crust. Whisk the eggs and half-and-half in a medium bowl until frothy and well combined, then season with salt and pepper. Pour into the crust.

Bake until set in the middle, about 40 to 45 minutes, covering the crust around the edges with foil if it starts to get too dark. Let the quiche sit for 5 to 10 minutes to set a bit more, then garnish with the scallions and any leftover herbs if desired. Slice into wedges to serve.

Finnish Oven Pancake with Ricotta Honey Whip, Peas, and Asparagus

(Pannukakku)

Pannukakku is a traditional Finnish dish similar to a Dutch baby pancake. It is usually a sweet dish topped with berries, jam, and sugar, but it can also be savory. I've done a bit of both here, combining fresh spring vegetables and jammy eggs with a sweet ricotta honey whip and honey mustard drizzle. It's so much fun to watch as the batter puffs up and turns golden in the skillet.

Makes 8 servings.

Pannukakku

5 eggs, room temperature, divided
1 cup whole milk, room temperature
3/4 cup all-purpose flour
1/2 teaspoon kosher salt, plus more to taste
3 tablespoons butter

Ricotta Honey Whip

1/2 cup ricotta
1 tablespoon olive oil
3 tablespoons honey, divided
1/2 teaspoon lemon zest (less than 1/2 lemon)
1 teaspoon freshly squeezed lemon juice (less than 1/2 lemon)
Kosher salt
Freshly ground black pepper

To Assemble the Pannukakku

1/2 cup thinly sliced asparagus spears, with tips reserved for garnish
1/2 cup fresh peas
5 or 6 fresh basil leaves
2 tablespoons sliced scallions
1/2 cup mayonnaise (store-bought or homemade using the recipe on page 89)
2 tablespoons whole-grain or coarse mustard
1/2 teaspoon champagne vinegar
Water
Olive oil for drizzling
Kosher salt
Freshley ground black pepper

For the Pannukakku

Whisk three of the eggs and the milk in a large bowl until well combined. In a small bowl whisk the flour and salt. Add the flour mixture to the egg mixture and whisk until smooth and no lumps remain. (I like to

recipe continues

continued from page 151

press my batter through a fine-mesh strainer to remove any lumps. You could also pulse it in your blender or immersion blender.) The batter will be thin and will look like pancake batter.

Let the batter sit for 10 to 15 minutes while you preheat the oven to 425 degrees. With about 5 minutes left of the resting time, add the butter to a 10-inch cast-iron skillet. Put the skillet in the oven for 4 to 5 minutes, until the butter melts. Swirl the pan to evenly cover the bottom of the pan with butter.

Once the batter has rested, pour it into the hot skillet and bake until your pannukakku is puffy and golden brown, about 16 to 18 minutes. Remove the pan from the oven and let cool for a few minutes.

While the pannukakku is baking, steam or soft-cook the remaining two eggs for 8 minutes (see page 30 for method), then set in a bowl of ice water until cool enough to peel. Carefully peel the eggs and set aside.

For the Ricotta Honey Whip

To make the ricotta whip, add the ricotta, olive oil, 1 tablespoon of the honey, lemon zest, and lemon juice to the bowl of a food processor or blender and puree until smooth and creamy. Season with salt and pepper.

To Assemble the Pannukakku

Spread the Ricotta Honey Whip on the warm pannukakku, then top with the asparagus, peas, basil, and scallions.

In a small bowl whisk the remaining 2 tablespoons honey with the mayonnaise, mustard, and vinegar until smooth. Add water one teaspoon at a time until you reach drizzling consistency. Carefully slice the eggs and arrange over the top of the pancake, then drizzle with the honey mustard dressing and additional olive oil if desired. Garnish with reserved asparagus tips and season with salt and pepper. Cut into slices or wedges and serve warm. Refrigerate leftovers.

Fresh Tip: Measure out the olive oil first. Then, if you use the same tablespoon for the honey, the honey will slide right out.

Creamy Baked Eggs with Parmesan, Black Olives, and Fresh Herbs

Baking eggs in cream results in a wonderful, almost custard-like consistency that is perfect for dipping buttered toast into. I prefer thin strips of a crusty rustic bread that can hold up to the herby freshness of the dish. I have suggested my favorite herb blend, but feel free to substitute your favorite herbs and even the cheese of your choice. The black olives lend a salty boost that I love.

Makes 3 servings.

2 tablespoons butter
1/4 cup heavy cream
6 eggs
2 cloves garlic, finely chopped
1/4 cup chopped black olives
1/4 cup chopped fresh herbs (tarragon, sage, parsley, thyme), plus more for garnish
1/4 cup grated Romano
Kosher salt
Freshly ground black pepper
Toasted buttered bread, cut into sticks for dipping

Preheat the broiler with the oven rack in the top position, about 6 inches from the heat. Add the butter and cream to a pie plate or oven-safe dish. Place under the broiler until bubbles form and the butter is melted, about 2 minutes.

Remove the pan from the oven and break the eggs into the cream, trying not to break the yolks. Sprinkle the garlic, olives, chopped herb blend, and Romano over the top. Season with salt and pepper.

Broil for another 6 to 7 minutes until the whites are set, the yolks are still runny, and the top is browned and bubbling (watch closely since broilers differ). Remove the pan from the oven and garnish with additional fresh herbs. Serve warm with buttered toast sticks for dipping.

Asparagus, Cheddar, and Scallion Frittata

Raw asparagus lends a satisfying crunch to this frittata that makes a quick and easy option for breakfast or a light lunch. Don't like asparagus? You can substitute green beans or peas instead. Regardless, it's such a wonderful way to showcase crisp and fresh spring produce.

Makes 4 to 6 servings.

2 tablespoons butter
5 eggs
1 cup thinly sliced fresh asparagus spears (about 15 spears), with the tips separated
1 small shallot, half cut into thin rings, half chopped
1 cup (4 ounces) shredded white Cheddar
2 scallions, thinly sliced, divided
Kosher salt
Freshly ground pepper
Olive oil for drizzling

Preheat the broiler with the rack in the upper third portion of the oven. Add the butter to an 8-inch skillet or oven-safe baking dish and set in the oven on the bottom rack for a minute or two until the butter melts.

In a medium bowl whisk the eggs until uniformly combined and frothy, then stir in the sliced asparagus spears, chopped shallot, Cheddar, half of the scallions, salt, and pepper.

Remove the skillet from the oven and pour the egg mixture into the pan. Cook on the stovetop over medium heat for 2 to 3 minutes to set the bottom, then remove from the heat.

Arrange the asparagus tips and shallot rings on top. Broil on the top rack for 3 to 4 minutes until the frittata is puffed, set in the middle, and browned around the edges. Let cool for a few minutes, then garnish with the remaining scallions, drizzle with olive oil, and cut into wedges.

Bacon, Egg, and Cheese French Toast Bake

This sweet-savory baked version of the French favorite is great for crowds or busy weekday mornings since you can prep and assemble it the night before and then pop it into the oven when you wake up. It's best to use slightly stale bread that will hold up better and absorb more of the batter, so leave a few slices out on the counter a day or so before you make this dish. This egg bake combines all your breakfast favorites—bacon, eggs, and cheese, plus a splash of orange juice—under a light dusting of powdered sugar. Yum!

Makes 9 to 12 servings.

6 slices thick-cut bacon
Freshly ground black pepper
8 eggs
1 1/2 cups whole milk
3 tablespoons freshly squeezed orange juice (about 1 orange)
1 teaspoon granulated sugar
1/2 teaspoon kosher salt
8 slices slightly stale sandwich bread
1 cup shredded white Cheddar (about 4 ounces)
Powdered sugar, for dusting
Maple syrup, for drizzling
Orange slices, for garnish

Preheat the oven to 375 degrees. In a 9 x 13-inch baking dish, arrange the bacon strips in the dish in a single layer, add a few grinds of pepper over the top, and bake for 25 minutes until partially but not fully cooked. Remove the bacon to a paper towel–lined plate to drain and drain any excess bacon grease from the dish.

In a large bowl, whisk the eggs, milk, orange juice, sugar, and salt. Season with more pepper. Dip each bread slice into the mixture, one at a time, coating both sides and allowing the liquid to seep into the bread. Then arrange the slices in the pan, slightly overlapping them.

Pour the remaining egg mixture over the bread slices and cover with the Cheddar. Cover the pan with plastic wrap and let it sit at room temperature for 1 hour to allow the bread to soak up more of the liquid (the pan can be refrigerated up to 2 days at this stage).

After soaking, heat the oven to 350 degrees. Arrange the bacon on top of the egg, bread, and cheese mixture, and bake uncovered for 40 to 45 minutes until the egg is set and puffed, the cheese is bubbling and melted, and the bacon is crispy.

Let cool slightly on a wire rack before slicing into squares and serving with a dusting of powdered sugar and a drizzle of maple syrup, garnishing with orange slices.

One-Pan Baked Creamy Eggs on Toast

(Oeufs au Plat Bressanne)

These sinfully creamy baked eggs on toast are adapted from a traditional French recipe. They're a great way to prepare breakfast for a crowd, coming together in just a few minutes with common ingredients. You can use any type of sandwich bread you wish, or even a brioche or rustic loaf. Day-old or slightly stale bread also works wonderfully in this recipe.

Makes 4 servings.

4 tablespoons butter, room temperature, plus more for greasing
4 slices bread
1 cup heavy cream
Kosher salt
Freshly ground black pepper
8 eggs
1 tablespoon thinly chopped fresh chives
1 tablespoon thinly chopped fresh chives, for garnish (optional)
Freshly grated nutmeg

Preheat the oven to 375 degrees. Grease a 9 x 13-inch casserole dish.

Generously butter the bread on both sides. Heat a medium skillet over medium-high heat, then toast the bread on both sides until crispy and golden, about a minute per side. Remove the bread from the skillet.

Pour half of the cream into the prepared baking dish, season with salt and pepper, then nestle the slices of bread on top. Carefully crack two eggs on top of each slice of toast (it's okay if the whites run over), then pour the remaining cream over the top. Season again with salt and pepper.

Bake for 14 or 15 minutes, until the cream is bubbly and has thickened slightly, the egg whites are set, and the yolks are still a bit runny (adjust the cooking time depending on how runny you like your yolks). Garnish with the chives if desired, season with additional pepper, then grate some nutmeg over the top and serve.

Best eaten warm the same day, but leftovers can be refrigerated and reheated.

Finnish Oven Pancakes with Caramelized Onions, Walnuts, and Fontina

(Pannukakku)

This version of the traditional Finnish dish is savory instead of sweet. I'm partial to the delicious caramelized onions, sherry, and melty Fontina cheese in this oven pancake. The onions will take a while to cook down and caramelize, but the effort will be well worth it. I've used four 6 1/2-inch cast-iron skillets to make individual servings, but you can also make one large pancake in a 10-inch oven-safe dish. Just be sure to increase your baking time to 15 to 18 minutes.

Makes 4 servings.

Onion and Walnut Filling

1 tablespoon butter
2 teaspoons olive oil
12 fresh sage leaves
2 medium yellow onions, peeled, halved, and thinly sliced (about 3 cups)
1/2 teaspoon kosher salt, plus more to taste
1 teaspoon granulated sugar
2 tablespoons sherry
Freshly ground black pepper
1/2 cup walnut pieces

Pannukakku

3 eggs
1 cup whole milk
3/4 cup all-purpose flour
1/2 teaspoon salt
3 tablespoons butter
3/4 cup shredded Fontina

For the Filling

In a large skillet over medium heat, heat the butter and olive oil until the butter is melted and the oil is shimmering. Add the sage leaves and fry for about 45 seconds until aromatic and crispy. Remove the leaves from the oil and drain on a paper towel–lined plate.

Add the onions to the pan, sprinkle the salt and sugar over them, then stir to coat evenly. Reduce the heat to medium-low and cook the onions, stirring occasionally, until they are deep golden brown, about 25 minutes. Add the sherry to the pan and scrape up any bits that are stuck to the bottom. Continue to cook and stir for another minute until the liquid is completely absorbed. Season with salt and pepper and remove to a plate.

Wipe out the skillet and heat over medium-high heat. Add the walnuts to the dry pan and cook for 4 to 5 minutes, stirring occasionally, until the nuts are aromatic and just starting to brown. Transfer to a plate to cool.

recipe continues

continued from page 163

For the Pannukakku

Whisk the eggs and milk in a medium bowl. In a small bowl whisk the flour and salt, then stir the dry ingredients into the egg mixture. Whisk the batter until smooth and no lumps remain (press the batter through a fine-mesh strainer, if desired). Let the batter rest for a bit.

Preheat the oven to 425 degrees. Divide the butter between four 6 1/2-inch cast-iron skillets (if you are making one large pancake, add all of the butter to your baking pan). Put the skillets in the oven for 4 to 5 minutes until the butter melts. Swirl the pans to evenly cover the bottoms with butter.

Divide the batter evenly into the hot skillets (about 1 cup each) and bake for 10 to 12 minutes (15 to 18 minutes for one large pannukakku) or until your pannukakku are puffed and light golden brown. Remove from the oven, spoon the caramelized onions on top, and then the Fontina. Return the pannukakku to the oven for 2 to 3 minutes more to allow the cheese to melt. Remove from the oven and garnish with the toasted walnuts and fried sage leaves. Serve warm.

Crunchy Baked Vanilla Bourbon French Toast Sticks

If you're not a big fan of French toast because it tends to be mushy in the middle, you'll love these baked French toast sticks. They come out crunchy and delicious every time! Plus, they're great when you're feeding a crowd because they all cook at once. The vanilla bourbon sauce adds just the right touch and makes them perfect for your next adult brunch. (Let the kids have some plain maple syrup to dunk theirs in.)

Makes 32 sticks.

Bourbon Dipping Sauce

Makes about 1 cup.

1/4 cup (1/2 stick) butter
1/2 cup firmly packed brown sugar
1/4 cup heavy cream
2 tablespoons bourbon
2 teaspoons vanilla bean paste
Pinch of salt

French Toast Sticks

8 slices thick-cut bread, such as brioche or challah
3 eggs
3/4 cup half-and-half
3 tablespoons bourbon
2 tablespoons firmly packed brown sugar
2 teaspoons vanilla bean paste
1 teaspoon ground cardamom
1/4 teaspoon freshly grated nutmeg
Pinch of salt
2 tablespoons granulated sugar, divided
Powdered sugar, for dusting

For the Sauce

Melt the butter in a saucepan over medium-low heat. Add the brown sugar and cream and whisk until the sugar has dissolved. Continue to simmer for 3 to 4 minutes, then remove from the heat and whisk in the bourbon, vanilla bean paste, and salt. Let cool slightly. The sauce will thicken up a bit as it cools.

For the French Toast Sticks

Preheat the oven to 350 degrees. Line a baking sheet with parchment paper. Cut each slice of bread into four 1-inch "sticks."

In a shallow bowl or loaf pan, whisk the eggs, half-and-half, bourbon, brown sugar, vanilla bean paste, cardamom, nutmeg, and salt.

Dip each breadstick into the egg mixture, one at a time, letting it soak up some of the liquid so all sides are covered but not so much that the bread falls apart. Allow the excess liquid to drip back into the bowl, then place the sticks on the prepared baking sheet, leaving space between each stick. Sprinkle 1 tablespoon of the granulated sugar over the sticks.

recipe continues

RÖSLE

continued from page 165

Bake the sticks for 15 minutes, then flip and sprinkle with the remaining 1 tablespoon sugar. Bake for an additional 15 minutes until golden brown on both sides. Dust with powdered sugar and serve with Bourbon Dipping Sauce.

Refrigerate leftovers and use within 3 or 4 days. Sticks can be reheated in a skillet over medium heat. Cook, turning a few times, until the sticks are warmed through and have crisped up again.

Egg and Mushroom Tart

This simple tart is great for a crowd and can be served any time of day. Cut it into slices for brunch, or serve up big squares alongside a salad for dinner. Don't like mushrooms? You can swap in other vegetables instead. Or just make an egg and cheese tart. It's a very versatile basic recipe that comes together quickly. I always keep a box or two of puff pastry in my freezer for this reason.

Makes 1 tart.

Flour for dusting
1 sheet frozen puff pastry, thawed
2 tablespoons butter
12 ounces button mushrooms, stemmed and sliced
2 cloves garlic, thinly sliced
1 shallot, finely chopped
2 teaspoons sherry
Kosher salt
Freshly ground black pepper
7 eggs, divided
1 1/2 cups shredded Fontina
1 scallion, thinly sliced, for garnish
Olive oil, for drizzling

Line a rimmed baking sheet with parchment paper. On a lightly floured surface, roll out the puff pastry into a 14 x 11-inch rectangle. Transfer it to the prepared baking sheet. Use a knife to score a 1/2-inch border around the edge of the pastry. Prick the pastry inside the border with a fork to prevent it from puffing in the center. Refrigerate the pastry while you prepare the topping, at least 20 minutes.

To make the topping, melt the butter in a large skillet over medium heat. Add the mushrooms, garlic, and shallot and cook, stirring occasionally, until starting to brown, about 10 minutes. Add the sherry and cook for another minute or so until the liquid is absorbed. Season with salt and pepper, and set aside.

Preheat the oven to 375 degrees. Whisk one of the eggs with 1 teaspoon water, then brush the pastry with the egg wash. Bake on the middle rack until puffed around the edges and light golden brown, about 14 minutes. Remove from the oven and press down on the center with a spatula if the pastry has puffed up.

Top the pastry with the cheese, then the mushroom mixture, staying within the border. Make a divot for each of the remaining six eggs in the topping with the back of a spoon, and carefully crack the eggs on top, spacing them out evenly.

Return the pan to the oven and bake until the pastry is deep golden and the egg whites are set, about 12 to 14 minutes (the egg yolks will still be runny). Sprinkle with the scallions, drizzle with olive oil, and cut into slices or squares.

Fresh Tip: Don't throw away the root end of the scallion. Instead, you can regrow it by putting it in a small glass of water. All you need is about an inch or so of scallion root. It will grow new greens several more times that you can snip off as needed.

Monte Cristo Breakfast Bake

Taking the flavors of a classic Monte Cristo sandwich—ham, turkey, mustard, and Swiss cheese—and transforming them into a hearty casserole perfect for a crowd, this breakfast bake can be assembled the night before and then popped into the oven the next morning. Dusting the top with powdered sugar and serving it alongside raspberry jam stays true to the traditional recipe and adds just the right hint of sweetness to an otherwise savory dish. I like to keep the cheeses and meats chunky, so I ask at the deli counter for 1/2-inch slices that I can then easily cut into uniform 1/2-inch cubes.

Makes 8 servings.

4 eggs
1 cup heavy cream
1/2 cup whole milk
1 tablespoon Dijon mustard
1/4 teaspoon freshly grated nutmeg
1/4 teaspoon freshly ground black pepper
Butter for greasing the dish
6 cups slightly stale cubed French bread, divided
1 cup cubed deli turkey (1/2-inch cubes, about 3 ounces)
1 cup cubed Black Forest or honey ham (1/2-inch cubes, about 3 ounces)
1 cup cubed Swiss (1/2-inch cubes, about 4 ounces)
1/2 cup Gruyère (1/2-inch cubes, about 2 ounces)
4 tablespoons raspberry jam, divided
1/4 cup (1/2 stick) salted butter, melted
Powdered sugar, for dusting

Whisk the eggs in a 2-cup liquid measuring cup. Whisk in the cream, milk, mustard, nutmeg, and pepper. Grease a 9 x 13-inch casserole dish and arrange half of the bread cubes in a single layer in the dish. Layer the turkey, ham, Swiss, and Gruyère on top of the bread. Dollop with 2 tablespoons of the jam. Pour the egg mixture over the top, then top with the remaining bread cubes. Cover with plastic wrap, pressing down to submerge the bread a bit, and refrigerate for at least 2 hours (or up to overnight).

When you're ready to cook, preheat the oven to 350 degrees. Remove the plastic wrap from the casserole, and bake for 20 minutes. Then remove from the oven, brush with the melted butter, then bake for another 10 to 15 minutes, until the cheese is bubbling and the top is golden brown. Remove the pan from the oven to cool and set for 10 to 15 minutes, then cut the bake into slices and put on plates. Dust the slices with powdered sugar.

In a small bowl whisk the remaining 2 tablespoons jam with 1 tablespoon water to thin. Serve with thinned raspberry jam on the side. Leftovers can be stored tightly covered in the refrigerator and briefly reheated in a warm oven.

Note: I generally don't add salt to this recipe. I feel that between the ham, turkey, and cheeses, plus the butter brushed on top, there's enough, but feel free to season to your taste.

Mini Charcuterie Stratas

Any combination of meats and cheese will work in this simple, easily customizable baked egg dish. You can use whatever types of cheese and breakfast meats you have on hand, so it's a great way to use up leftovers from a cheese or charcuterie board during the holidays. Any kind of bread will do, but I prefer to use a nice rustic loaf, sourdough, or ciabatta rolls. And the older the bread, the better. Stale bread works fine in this recipe, as it does for most baked egg recipes.

Makes 12 stratas.

3 cups bread, cut into 1/2-inch cubes
1 cup cooked, chopped breakfast sausage, pepperoni, or chorizo, or a combination
1 cup cubed cheese, such as Cheddar, Gruyère, Fontina, or a combination (about 4 ounces)
12 eggs
1/2 cup heavy cream
1/2 teaspoon kosher salt, plus more to taste
1/4 teaspoon freshly grated nutmeg
1/4 teaspoon freshly ground black pepper
1/4 cup sliced scallions

Preheat the oven to 375 degrees. Line a 12-cup muffin tin with liners or spray the pan with cooking spray.

Divide the bread cubes between the cups. Add the chopped meat and cheese.

In a medium bowl whisk the eggs, cream, salt, nutmeg, and pepper. Pour the egg mixture over the meats and cheese, then top with the scallions. Let sit for about 30 minutes as the oven heats, which will allow the bread to soak up some of the egg mixture.

When the oven has heated, bake the stratas on the middle rack until the centers have set and the tops are puffed and golden brown, about 25 to 30 minutes. Let sit for several minutes to cool, then serve warm.

OMELETS AND QUESADILLAS

Smoked Gouda Egg Quesadilla with Baby Spinach

This quesadilla recipe couldn't be easier because it's all cooked in one pan—in mere minutes! I love a good smoked Gouda, but you can certainly experiment with other types of cheese. The spinach is optional, but it adds a nice boost of nutrition, not to mention flavor, to this quick breakfast, which is perfect for a lazy weekend or weekdays before school.

Makes 1 serving.

2 eggs
1 tablespoon butter
Kosher salt
Freshly ground black pepper
1/2 cup fresh baby spinach
1/4 cup shredded smoked Gouda
8-inch flour tortilla

Whisk the eggs in a small bowl until smooth and well combined. Melt the butter in a medium skillet over low heat. When the butter stops sizzling, add the eggs. Season with salt and pepper, then top with the spinach and Gouda.

Let the eggs cook, without stirring in the spinach and cheese, until the egg is mostly set, about 2 minutes. Place the tortilla onto the spinach and cheese and press gently. Slide a wide spatula or fish turner under the egg to loosen it from the pan, then carefully flip the whole thing over. Let cook for another minute or two until the tortilla is crispy and golden brown in spots.

Remove the pan from the heat and use a spatula to slide the tortilla onto a cutting board. Fold the tortilla in half, then cut it into three wedges and serve warm.

Avocado and Goat Cheese Breakfast Quesadillas

Creamy avocado and goat cheese, piled into a quesadilla with cooked eggs, are the ultimate breakfast comfort food. Lime adds bright notes, and the cilantro offers a nice earthy, herbaceous flavor for fans of cilantro. If you don't like cilantro, either substitute with parsley or leave it off entirely.

Makes 2 servings.

4 eggs, divided
Kosher salt
Freshly ground black pepper
2 to 3 tablespoons butter, divided
1 avocado
4 (6-inch) flour tortillas
Juice from one lime
4 ounces goat cheese, crumbled (about 1/2 cup)
2 sprigs fresh cilantro, roughly chopped, reserving some for the garnish (optional)

Whisk two of the eggs in a small bowl and season with salt and pepper. Heat 1 tablespoon of the butter in a medium skillet over medium-low heat and cook the eggs, tilting the pan to cover the bottom evenly (almost like you're making an omelet). Slide the eggs onto a plate, and repeat with the remaining two eggs, adding more butter if necessary.

Use a fork to mash the avocado and divide it between two of the tortillas. Squeeze some lime juice over the avocado. Top the avocado with the goat cheese, then top with the eggs, some cilantro, and the remaining tortillas.

Wipe out the skillet and melt the remaining 1 tablespoon butter over medium-low heat. Cook the quesadillas, one at a time, about 1 minute on each side, pressing down a bit on the top, carefully flipping halfway through so both sides are lightly browned.

Cut each into quarters and garnish with the remaining cilantro.

Fresh Tip: You can check an avocado's ripeness by removing the stem. If the flesh underneath is pale green, the avocado isn't ripe yet. If it's brown or black, the avocado is probably past its prime. You want to see nice bright green flesh under there. A green Haas avocado isn't ripe yet; you want to wait until it turns a deep, dark green. A ripe avocado will yield slightly when you squeeze it. You can slow an avocado's ripening by sticking it in the refrigerator or speed it up by putting it in a paper bag with a banana or apple.

French Omelets with Bleu Cheese and Chives

I've taken a classic French trifold omelet and filled it with two traditional French flavors: bleu cheese and chives. If you're lucky enough to have wild chives growing in your garden (or yard!), this is a great vehicle for them. I often use yard chives in recipes when I don't have scallions (just rinse them well first). As for seasoning, the cheese is salty enough that I don't think this omelet needs more salt, but by all means, season it as you see fit.

Makes 2 omelets.

4 eggs, room temperature, divided
2 teaspoons oil of choice, divided, plus more for drizzling
2 tablespoons butter, divided
2 ounces bleu cheese, crumbled (about 1/2 cup), divided
2 teaspoons chopped fresh chives, divided, plus more for garnish
Freshly ground black pepper

Heat a 9- or 10-inch omelet pan or shallow skillet with sloped sides over medium-high heat. Whisk two of the eggs in a small bowl until combined. Add 1 teaspoon of the oil to the pan and tilt it to coat the bottom. Then add 1 tablespoon of the butter and swirl it around the pan.

Once the butter has melted and is foamy, pour the eggs into the pan. Tilt the pan to spread the egg evenly, for about 45 to 60 seconds.

When the egg is mostly set, but the bottom hasn't started to brown, shake the pan or run a rubber spatula around the edge and underneath to loosen the eggs, then sprinkle half the bleu cheese down the center of the omelet. Then add half the chives.

Tilt the pan and, using the spatula, fold over two sides of the omelet toward the center. Slide the omelet onto a plate, carefully flipping it over so the seam is on the bottom.

Repeat for the second omelet, then garnish the omelets with the additional chives, pepper, and a drizzle of oil, if desired.

Omelet Variations

Here are some herb and cheese pairings that I also love:

Gruyère and tarragon
Swiss and dill
Goat cheese and basil
Cheddar and rosemary
Gouda and sage

Fiesta Egg and Vegetable Quesadillas

These festive quesadillas will make breakfast a celebration and will start your day off right with a medley of fresh vegetables and eggs. Combining all your favorite quesadilla flavors, it's a party on a plate! For even more fun, lay out all the toppings in separate bowls and let everyone garnish their own quesadillas.

Makes 2 servings.

3 to 4 tablespoons butter, divided
4 eggs, room temperature, divided
1/2 cup sour cream, room temperature, divided
Kosher salt
Freshly ground black pepper
2 (8-inch) flour tortillas
Kosher salt
Freshly ground black pepper
1/2 cup shredded mozzarella, divided
1/2 cup shredded Cheddar, divided
1/2 medium red onion, minced, divided
2 scallions, thinly sliced, whites and greens separated, divided
1 medium tomato, diced, divided
1 avocado, peeled, pitted, and diced, divided
1/2 cup chopped black olives, divided
1 teaspoon hot pepper sauce
1 teaspoon lime zest (about 1/2 lime)
1 teaspoon freshly squeezed lime juice (less than 1/2 lime)

Heat 1 tablespoon of the butter in a medium skillet over medium-low heat. Whisk two of the eggs and 2 tablespoons of the sour cream in a small bowl, then season with salt and pepper and pour into the pan. Cook the eggs, tilting the pan to cover the bottom evenly (almost like you're making an omelet). Slide the eggs onto a plate, and repeat with the remaining two eggs and 2 tablespoons sour cream, adding more butter if necessary. Wipe the skillet out and set aside.

Lay the tortillas on a flat surface. Divide half of the mozzarella and Cheddar between the two tortillas, sprinkling cheese on one side of each. Pile the cooked egg mixture on top of the cheese. Reserving a bit of each to use as a garnish, top with the onion, white parts of the scallion, tomato, avocado, and olives. Then finish with the remainder of the mozzarella and Cheddar. Fold each tortilla in half and press to flatten slightly.

Melt 1 tablespoon of the butter in the skillet over low heat, then cook one quesadilla until golden brown on the bottom. Carefully flip the quesadilla over and cook the other side. Repeat with the second quesadilla, adding the remaining 1 tablespoon butter if needed.

Cut each quesadilla into thirds, creating three wedges, and arrange on plates.

In a separate small bowl whisk 2 tablespoons of the remaining sour cream with the hot sauce and 1 teaspoon water, adding more water if necessary, until the sauce is drizzling consistency.

In a small bowl make a lime crema dipping sauce by whisking the remaining sour cream with the lime zest and lime juice. Season with pepper, and divide between two small pinch bowls. Garnish the quesadillas with some of the reserved red onion, scallions, and olives, if desired, and serve the lime crema on the side.

Mushroom Goat Cheese Omelets with Crispy Shallots and Sage

Hearty flavors of mushrooms and goat cheese burst forth with each savory bite of this omelet. And the crispy, caramelized topping lends a nice crunch to the smooth, silky goat cheese filling. The shallots do take a while to cook, but it's well worth the wait.

Makes 2 omelets.

Crispy Shallots and Sage

1 tablespoon olive oil
1 small shallot, thinly sliced
8 to 10 fresh sage leaves
Kosher salt
Freshly ground black pepper

Mushroom Goat Cheese Omelets

4 ounces Baby Bella mushrooms, cut into quarters
1 teaspoon sherry (optional)
Kosher salt
Freshly ground black pepper
1 tablespoon butter, divided
1 tablespoon olive oil, divided, plus more for drizzling
4 eggs, divided
2 ounces goat cheese, crumbled (about 1/4 cup), divided

For the Crispy Shallots and Sage

Heat the olive oil in an omelet pan or 8- or 9-inch skillet with sloped sides over medium-low heat. Add the shallots and sage leaves and cook, stirring occasionally, until the shallots are crispy and evenly browned, about 8 minutes. Turn down the heat if the shallots are browning too quickly or starting to burn. Season with salt and pepper to taste, and transfer them to a paper towel–lined plate.

For the Omelets

Increase the heat to medium-high and add the mushrooms to the same skillet, cut side down. Cook for several minutes, without stirring, until the mushrooms are golden brown on one side and the liquid has evaporated. Add the sherry, if using, and season with salt and pepper. Cook, stirring, for another minute or two, then remove the mushrooms to a plate.

Add half the butter and olive oil to the skillet and reduce the heat to low. Whisk two eggs in a small bowl and season with salt and pepper. When the butter in the pan starts to foam and bubble, add the eggs. Tilt the pan to spread the egg evenly, for about 45 to 60 seconds.

When the egg is mostly set, shake the pan or run a rubber spatula around the edge and underneath to loosen the eggs, then spoon half the goat cheese down the center of the omelet. Top with half the mushrooms, then tilt the pan and, using a spatula, fold over two sides of the omelet. Slide the omelet onto a plate, then top with half of the fried shallots and sage.

Repeat for the second omelet. Drizzle the omelets with additional olive oil, if desired, and season with salt and pepper.

Cheesy Bacon and Egg Breakfast Tortillas

This delicious breakfast dish turns a traditional bacon, egg, and cheese sandwich on its head, piling everything onto flour tortillas that are browned in a hot skillet until they're crispy and light golden on the bottom and melty on top.

Makes 2 servings.

4 eggs, divided
Kosher salt
Freshly ground black pepper
1 to 2 tablespoons butter, divided
2 (6-inch) flour tortillas
1 tablespoon neutral oil
4 slices cooked bacon
1/2 cup shredded Fontina
2 tablespoons grated Parmesan
1 tablespoon chopped fresh dill, plus more for garnish

Whisk two of the eggs in a medium bowl and season with salt and pepper. Heat 1 tablespoon of the butter in a medium skillet over medium-low heat and cook the eggs, tilting the pan to cover the bottom evenly (almost like you're making an omelet). Slide the eggs onto a plate, and repeat with the remaining two eggs, adding more butter if necessary. Divide the cooked eggs between the two tortillas. Top each with 2 slices of bacon. Then sprinkle the Fontina, Parmesan, and dill over the top.

Wipe out the skillet and heat the oil over medium heat. Cook the tortillas with the toppings on top, one at a time, for about 1 minute, until golden on the bottom and the cheeses are melted. Cut each into quarters and serve garnished with the remaining dill.

IN SEASON — WINTER

Cream Cheese and Lox Omelets with Capers and Dill

Enjoy all the flavors of your favorite bagel without all the carbs! Like my other omelets, I like to line up the filling for this omelet down the middle of the pan and then fold over both sides for a more elegant presentation, but you can arrange the filling on one side and then just fold the omelet in half if that's easier for you.

Makes 2 omelets.

- 4 eggs, room temperature, divided
- 2 teaspoons oil of choice, plus more for drizzling, divided
- 2 tablespoons butter, divided
- 2 slices smoked salmon, cut into small pieces (about 2 ounces), divided
- 2 ounces cream cheese, cut into small cubes, divided
- 2 thin slices of red onion, separated into rings, divided
- 2 tablespoons capers, plus more for garnish, divided
- 2 sprigs fresh dill, for garnish

Heat a 9- or 10-inch omelet pan or shallow skillet with sloped sides over medium-high heat. In a small bowl whisk two of the eggs until combined. Add 1 teaspoon of the oil to the pan and tilt it to coat the bottom. Then add 1 tablespoon of the butter and swirl it around the pan.

Once the butter has melted and is foamy, pour the eggs into the pan. Tilt the pan to spread the egg evenly, for about 45 to 60 seconds.

When the eggs are almost set, arrange half of the smoked salmon, cream cheese, onion, and capers down the middle of the pan. Then tilt the skillet and, using the tip of a spatula, work around the edges, pull the eggs away from the pan to loosen them. Fold one side of the omelet over toward the center, tilt the pan the other way, and fold over the other side. Slide your omelet out of the pan and onto a plate.

Repeat for the second omelet, then garnish the omelets with the additional capers, fresh dill, and a drizzle of oil, if desired.

DEVILED EGGS

Savory

Green Goddess Deviled Eggs

Deep-Fried Deviled Eggs with Tarragon

Jammy Dressed Egg Flight

Caesar Deviled Eggs

Garlic Oeufs Mayonnaise
(Eggs with Mayo)

Eggs Jeanette

Smoked Salmon and Dill Holiday Deviled Eggs

Sweet

Elegant Honeydew and Prosciutto-Rose Eggs

Piña Colada Deviled Eggs

Black Forest Deviled Eggs

Green Goddess Deviled Eggs

Green goddess dressing, which relies heavily on fresh aromatic herbs and tangy sour cream, pairs perfectly with the egg yolks to create a garlicky, herby plate of deviled eggs that will be welcome at any picnic or potluck. These eggs actually taste better the second day, once the flavors have had time to meld together, so feel free to make them a day in advance.

Makes 12.

6 eggs, hard-cooked, peeled, and halved crossswise (see page 30 for method)
3/4 cup mayonnaise (store-bought or homemade using the recipe on page 89)
1/4 cup sour cream
1/2 teaspoon lemon zest, plus more for garnish (less than 1/2 lemon)
1 teaspoon freshly squeezed lemon juice (less than 1/2 lemon)
2 cloves garlic, roughly chopped
1/4 cup roughly chopped fresh basil leaves
2 tablespoons roughly chopped fresh tarragon leaves
2 tablespoons chopped fresh chives
2 tablespoons chopped scallion greens
Kosher salt
Freshly ground white pepper
12 baby basil leaves, for garnish

Carefully scoop the yolks out of the halved eggs and arrange the empty egg white halves on an egg tray.

Add the yolks to the bowl of a food processor, then add the mayonnaise, sour cream, lemon zest and juice, garlic, basil, tarragon, chives, and scallions and pulse until combined. Season to taste with salt and pepper. Continue to blend until the filling is smooth and creamy.

Using a 1/2-inch round piping tip and bag, generously pipe filling into each egg half. Garnish each egg with a baby basil leaf and additional lemon zest and pepper, if desired.

Serve immediately or chill until ready to serve. Leftovers should be stored in the refrigerator and eaten within 3 or 4 days.

Fresh Tip: Be sure to hang on to any extra fresh herbs, storing them for later use using the tips on pages 17–19.

Deep-Fried Deviled Eggs with Tarragon

This is a fun twist on a classic that will be a hit at your next potluck or barbeque. They're a perennial favorite—deviled eggs—but the whites are rolled in panko breadcrumbs and then fried before being finished with a subtle tarragon-scented filling. I love the pairing of tarragon with eggs, but you can substitute any herb you prefer. Dill, basil, and thyme also work great.

Makes 12.

Deep-Fried Eggs

Cooking oil for frying
6 eggs, hard-cooked, peeled, and halved lengthwise (see page 30 for method)
1 raw egg
1/4 cup all-purpose flour
3/4 cup panko breadcrumbs
Kosher salt
Freshly ground black pepper
1 tablespoon fresh minced tarragon (or 1 teaspoon dried), plus more for garnish

Filling

1/4 cup mayonnaise (store-bought or homemade using the recipe on page 89)
2 ounces mascarpone (about 1/4 cup)
1 ounce shredded Gruyère (about 2 tablespoons)
1 tablespoon freshly squeezed lemon juice (about 1/2 lemon)
Kosher salt
Freshly ground black pepper

For the Deep-Fried Eggs

Heat about 2 inches of cooking oil to 350 degrees in a heavy pot with steep sides. Meanwhile, remove the egg yolks to a medium bowl. In a small bowl lightly whisk the raw egg. In separate shallow bowls, measure out the flour and breadcrumbs. Season both with salt and pepper, then stir the tarragon into the breadcrumbs.

Carefully dip each cooked egg white into the flour, then the raw egg, and finally the breadcrumbs, pressing so the crumbs adhere to the surface evenly without breaking the egg white. In two batches, using a slotted spoon or small wire mesh strainer, carefully lower each breaded egg white into the oil and fry for about 30 seconds until evenly golden brown. Using the slotted spoon or strainer, remove the egg white halves from the oil and set them on a paper towel–lined plate to drain.

For the Filling

Mash the egg yolks in the bowl with a fork, then add the mayonnaise, mascarpone, Gruyère, and lemon juice and mix with a fork or potato masher until smooth. (Alternatively, place all the ingredients in a food processor and pulse until smooth.) Season to taste with salt and pepper, then, using a small ice-cream scoop or teaspoon, divide the filling between the egg whites. Garnish with additional tarragon and pepper.

Fresh Tip: I always like to cook up an extra egg or two when I'm making deviled eggs. That gives me a few extra whites to choose from in case they all don't peel well, and adding the extra yolks to the filling ensures that I have plenty to fill each half generously. Not to mention, since there's extra, I can taste as I go along.

Jammy Dressed Egg Flight

I first ran across "dressed" eggs in *How to Dress an Egg* by Ned Baldwin and Peter Kaminsky. I was researching a traditional French egg preparation called *oeufs* mayonnaise and in the process discovered dressed eggs. Basically, they're deviled eggs that eliminate scooping out the yolks and mashing them with the other ingredients. Instead, they call for leaving the slightly runny, jammy yolks in the egg halves, then topping them off with all kinds of interesting ingredients. Since my discovery, "egg flights" have gone sort of viral, but most call for hard-cooked eggs. I maintain that a jammy egg is what makes these flights soar (pun intended). The runny yolk mixes with the variety of toppings for the perfect bite.

Makes 12.

6 eggs
Toppings of your choice (see variations on the next page)

To cook the eggs, heat unsalted water to a boil in a large pot, then turn the heat down, bringing the water to a vigorous simmer. Set a colander, double boiler, vegetable steamer, or bamboo steamer on the pot so it rests above the water.

Rinse your eggs in warm water, then place them in the top of the steamer, making sure to leave room between them. You don't want to crowd the eggs, or they won't cook evenly. Cover and steam the eggs for 8 minutes, then, using tongs, gently set each egg into a large bowl of ice water until they are cool enough to peel.

Carefully crack the wide end of the egg and peel off the shell, being careful not to break the egg since the middle will still be liquid. Cut each egg in half lengthwise and set each half in an egg tray or on a platter. Garnish with toppings of your choice. The only limit is your imagination.

A Dozen Variations

Avocado
Avocado, mashed
Lime juice
Scallions, sliced
Freshly ground black pepper

Bacon Bleu Cheese Balsamic
Bacon, cooked until crisp, then crumbled
Bleu cheese, crumbled
Balsamic vinegar, for drizzling

Buffalo Bleu Cheese
Bleu cheese, crumbled
Celery, minced
Buffalo sauce

Caesar
Mayonnaise
Shredded lettuce
Lemon juice and zest
Panko breadcrumbs
Parmesan, grated

Chili Bacon
Chili crisp
Bacon, cooked until crisp, then crumbled
Chili oil, for drizzling
Freshly ground black pepper

Chili Crisp
Sriracha mayo (page 103)
Chili crisp, for drizzling
Panko breadcrumbs

Herb
Mayonnaise
Scallions
Fresh dill
Pink Himalayan sea salt

Olive and Onion
Kalamata, black, and green olives, chopped
Red onion, minced
Freshly ground black pepper
Panko breadcrumbs
Olive oil, for drizzling

Pesto
Pesto
Walnuts, chopped
Parmesan curls
Walnut oil, for drizzling

Smoked Salmon
Smoked salmon
Crème fraîche
Capers
Fresh dill
Lemon zest

Sriracha
Mayonnaise
Scallions
Black sesame seeds
Sriracha hot sauce

Sundried Tomato
Sundried tomatoes, chopped
Hot Honey Mayo (page 61), for drizzling
Fresh parsley
Chili flakes

Caesar Deviled Eggs

A classic salad, but make it deviled eggs. You'll recognize all the flavors of a traditional Caesar in each delicious bite of my deviled eggs, right down to the miniature garlic butter croutons on top of each one. These are so much fun to make—and even more fun to eat!

Makes 12.

- 6 eggs, hard-cooked, peeled, and halved lengthwise (see page 30 for method)
- 4 tablespoons mayonnaise (store-bought or homemade using the recipe on page 89), divided
- 2 teaspoons stone ground mustard
- 2 cloves garlic, minced
- 3 tablespoons grated Parmesan, plus 12 curls for garnish (optional)
- 1/4 teaspoon anchovy paste
- 1/2 teaspoon lemon zest (less than 1/2 lemon)
- 4 teaspoons freshly squeezed lemon juice, divided (about 1/2 lemon)
- Freshly ground black pepper
- 1 teaspoon butter
- Slice of bread, cut into 24 (1/4-inch) cubes
- Pinch of garlic powder
- 2 tablespoons shredded romaine lettuce

In the bowl of a food processor add the egg yolks, 3 tablespoons of the mayonnaise, mustard, garlic, grated Parmesan, anchovy paste, lemon zest, 2 teaspoons of the lemon juice, and a few grinds of pepper. Pulse until combined, scraping the sides of the bowl as necessary. Slowly add 2 to 3 teaspoons water and continue pulsing until the filling is smooth and creamy. (Alternatively, you can mash the yolks and mix the filling with a fork or potato masher.)

Arrange the egg whites on a plate and, using a pastry bag fitted with a 1/2-inch round tip, pipe the filling into the whites.

In a small saucepan over low heat, melt the butter, then gently stir in the bread cubes and toast, stirring occasionally, until golden brown, about 2 minutes. Remove the croutons from the heat and toss with the garlic powder.

In a small bowl whisk the remaining 1 tablespoon mayonnaise with the remaining 2 teaspoons lemon juice until smooth.

Garnish the eggs with the shredded romaine, garlic mini croutons, and Parmesan curls, if using. Drizzle with the lemon mayonnaise and season with pepper.

Serve immediately or chill until ready to serve. Leftovers should be stored in the refrigerator and eaten within 3 or 4 days.

Fresh Tip: Save uneaten deviled eggs and chop them up into a delicious egg salad for the next day.

Garlic Oeufs Mayonnaise

(Eggs with Mayo)

While not a classic filled deviled egg, this common French bistro hors d'oeuvre is quite honestly nothing more than a hard-cooked egg with mayonnaise (preferably homemade!) poured over the top. And I'm here for it! The traditional recipe calls for the egg halves to be arranged dome side up and for the mayonnaise to be a thin, pourable consistency, but personally I prefer a jammy egg yolk peeking out from under prettily piped topping. I also add some garlic to the mayonnaise, but you can omit that if you wish.

Makes 12.

Olive oil
2 cloves garlic, sliced
Kosher salt
6 eggs, soft-cooked, peeled, and halved lengthwise (see page 30 for method)
12 baby spinach leaves
1/2 cup mayonnaise (store-bought or homemade using the recipe on page 89)
Chopped fresh chives, for garnish
Chopped fresh tarragon, for garnish

Heat 1 tablespoon olive oil in a skillet over medium heat. When the oil is shimmering, add the garlic slices and cook until browned and crispy. Use tongs to remove the slices to a paper towel–lined plate. Once drained, mince, then season with salt.

Set each egg half on a spinach leaf on a plate, using a dab of mayonnaise to set each egg white in place, if necessary.

In a small bowl whisk the minced garlic into the mayonnaise, thinning the mixture with some warm water if necessary to achieve piping consistency, then season with salt. Using a pastry bag fitted with a star tip, pipe the garlic mayonnaise onto each egg.

Garnish with the chopped chives and tarragon and a sprinkle of salt.

Serve immediately or chill until ready to serve. Leftovers should be stored in the refrigerator and eaten within 3 or 4 days.

Fun fact: While deviled eggs date back to thirteenth-century Rome, mayonnaise wasn't invented until the mid-1700s and wasn't widely available commercially until the 1920s, so early recipes called for a raw egg yolk to bind the filling instead.

Eggs Jeanette

This recipe is my take on legendary chef Jacques Pépin's version of Eggs Jeanette, which he credits to his mother, Jeanette. Simple deviled eggs are fried then served with a silky mustard vinaigrette. I've subbed in tarragon for the parsley (of course!) and added some lemon juice as slight deviations from the original recipe, but I retained the overall look and feel of the dish.

Makes 12.

Eggs Jeanette

6 eggs, hard-cooked, peeled, and halved lengthwise (see page 30 for method)
2 tablespoons whole milk
1 clove garlic, finely chopped
2 teaspoons chopped fresh tarragon, plus more for garnish
1/4 teaspoon kosher salt
Freshly ground black pepper

Dressing

1 teaspoon Dijon mustard
2 teaspoons freshly squeezed lemon juice (about 1/2 lemon)
1/4 cup olive oil
Kosher salt

Assembly

2 tablespoons olive oil
Freshly ground black pepper
Tarragon, for garnish

For the Eggs

Using a spoon, carefully remove the yolks from the eggs and place the yolks in a medium bowl. Add the milk, garlic, tarragon, salt, and pepper. Mash with a fork until well combined. Reserve 2 tablespoons of the filling to use in the dressing. Spoon the remaining mixture into the egg whites, pressing and smoothing the filling flat.

For the Dressing

Add the mustard, lemon juice, and 1 tablespoon water to the bowl with the reserved filling and whisk until combined. Slowly drizzle in the oil while continuing to whisk until smooth. Season to taste with salt. Pour a pool of the dressing onto a serving plate, reserving some dressing for drizzling the eggs.

To Assemble the Eggs Jeanette

Heat the oil in a skillet over medium heat. When the oil is shimmering, place the eggs into the pan, stuffed side down. If necessary, work in batches. Fry until the eggs are evenly browned on the stuffed side, about 2 minutes. Using a spatula, remove the eggs from the oil and set filling side up on the plate of dressing, then drizzle the remaining dressing over the warm eggs. Garnish with pepper and tarragon, and serve.

Smoked Salmon and Dill Holiday Deviled Eggs

These deviled eggs are a personal favorite of mine—not only because they combine the flavors of cream cheese, dill, and lox, but also because they're so festive with the pink peppercorns and green dill (and if you add the panko breadcrumbs on top, it resembles newly fallen snow). Bring these to a holiday potluck, and you'll always return home with an empty dish.

Makes 12.

6 eggs, hard-cooked, peeled, and halved lengthwise (see page 30 for method)
2 ounces cream cheese, room temperature
Juice from 1 lemon
2 tablespoons whole milk
Kosher salt
Freshly ground white pepper
2 slices smoked salmon (about 2 ounces)
1 tablespoon chopped fresh dill, for garnish
1 teaspoon whole pink peppercorns, for garnish
1 teaspoon panko breadcrumbs, for garnish (optional)

Carefully scoop out the egg yolks and add to the bowl of a food processor. Arrange the empty egg white halves on an egg tray.

To the yolks, add the cream cheese, lemon juice, and milk and pulse to combine. Season to taste with salt and white pepper. Continue to blend until the filling is smooth and creamy. (Alternatively, you can use a fork or potato masher to blend the filling.)

Line each egg white with some of the salmon. Then, using a 1/2-inch piping tip and bag, pipe filling into each. Garnish the eggs with some fresh dill, peppercorns, and panko breadcrumbs, if desired.

Serve immediately or chill until ready to serve. Leftovers should be stored in the refrigerator and eaten within 3 or 4 days.

Elegant Honeydew and Prosciutto-Rose Eggs

Who says deviled eggs can only be savory? These delicately sweet bites have to be the most elegant version of deviled eggs I've ever made. And they're deceptively easy. Soft-cooked eggs are topped with a slice of juicy honeydew melon, a pretty prosciutto rose, and a sprig of fresh thyme for a fancy addition to your Easter or Mother's Day table.

Makes 12.

6 eggs, soft-cooked, peeled, and halved crosswise (see page 30 for method)
2 or 3 thin slices honeydew melon
1/2 cup mayonnaise (store-bought or homemade using the recipe on page 89)
1/2 teaspoon honey
2 slices prosciutto
1 to 2 fresh thyme sprigs, broken into small clusters.

Set each egg half on an egg plate. Cut out twelve 1-inch circles from the honeydew slices using a small round cookie cutter or the rim of a shot glass. Set one melon round on each egg half.

Whisk the mayonnaise and honey and, using a pastry bag fitted with a star tip, pipe the honey mayonnaise on top.

Leaving the prosciutto on the plastic sheets it came in, cut each slice crosswise into 1/2-inch lengths, then cut each length in half the long way. Roll up each piece to resemble a rose. Garnish each egg with a prosciutto rose and a small cluster of thyme leaves.

Serve immediately or chill until ready to serve. Leftovers should be stored in the refrigerator and eaten within 3 or 4 days.

Fresh Tip: If you don't have an egg tray, smear a dab of mayonnaise under each egg half on a platter to keep your eggs from sliding around.

Piña Colada Deviled Eggs

I had a lot of fun creating this recipe! I've put all the tropical flavors of a piña colada—coconut, pineapple, and maraschino cherries—into a sweet version of a deviled egg. It's boozy just like the real thing, but you can omit the coconut rum and use additional coconut cream instead to make a non-alcoholic version.

Makes 12.

- 1/4 cup unsweetened shredded coconut
- 2 tablespoons plus 1 teaspoon powdered sugar, divided
- 6 eggs, hard-cooked, peeled, and halved lengthwise (see page 30 for method)
- 3 tablespoons pineapple juice
- 2 tablespoons heavy cream or coconut cream
- 3 teaspoons coconut rum
- 12 maraschino cherries, drained on a paper towel and patted dry

Preheat the oven to 325 degrees. Line a baking sheet with parchment paper. Spread the shredded coconut flakes in an even layer and bake for 3 minutes, then stir them and bake for another 2 to 3 minutes until they're golden brown. Let cool, then toss with 1 teaspoon of the powdered sugar.

Add the egg yolks, pineapple juice, cream, and rum to the bowl of a food processor. Pulse until combined, scraping the sides of the bowl as necessary. Add the remaining 2 tablespoons powdered sugar and mix until smooth. Scrape down the sides of the bowl again and pulse a few more times. (Alternatively, you can mash the ingredients with a fork or potato masher until very creamy and smooth.)

Arrange the egg white halves on a plate and, using a pastry bag fitted with a 1/2-inch round tip, pipe the filling into the whites. Garnish each egg with toasted coconut and a cherry.

Serve immediately or chill until ready to serve. Leftovers should be stored in the refrigerator and eaten within 3 or 4 days.

Black Forest Deviled Eggs

These sweet deviled eggs will surprise you with all the well-loved flavors of a Black Forest cake. The chocolate, cocoa, and vanilla all combine into one luscious creamy bite—with a cherry on top.

Makes 12.

- 6 eggs, hard-cooked, peeled, and halved lengthwise (see page 30 for method)
- 2 ounces cream cheese, room temperature
- 2 tablespoons whole milk
- 1 teaspoon vanilla bean paste
- 1 tablespoon unsweetened cocoa powder
- 3 tablespoons plus 1 teaspoon powdered sugar, divided
- 1/8 teaspoon kosher salt
- 1/4 cup heavy cream
- 1 ounce milk or dark chocolate bar, for garnish
- 12 dark sweet cherries, fresh or from a jar, for garnish

Add the egg yolks, cream cheese, milk, and vanilla bean paste to the bowl of a food processor. Pulse until combined, scraping the sides of the bowl as necessary. Add the cocoa powder, 3 tablespoons of the powdered sugar, and salt and mix until smooth. Scrape down the sides of the bowl one last time and pulse a few more times. (Alternatively, use a fork or potato masher to combine the filling.)

To make the toppings, in the bowl of a stand mixer fitted with the whisk attachment, whip the heavy cream and the remaining teaspoon powdered sugar until stiff peaks form. Shave small curls from the chocolate bar with a vegetable peeler onto a small plate.

Arrange the egg white halves on a plate and, using a pastry bag fitted with a 1/2-inch round tip, pipe the chocolate filling into the whites. Fill another pastry bag with the whipped cream, and use a star tip to pipe it on top of the filling. Garnish each egg with a cherry and chocolate curls.

Serve immediately or chill until ready to serve. Leftovers should be stored in the refrigerator and eaten within 3 or 4 days.

BERRIES AND FRUIT

Strawberry Cardamom Cream Cheese Crepes

One-Bowl Strawberry Scones with Almond Drizzle

Glazed Cardamom Peach Quick Bread

Grilled Apricot and Burrata Caprese with Honey and Herb Oil

Maine Wild Blueberry Pie

Pretty in Pink Raspberry Party Cupcakes

Mixed Berry Brown Sugar Crumble

Roasted Grapes with Walnuts, Feta, Rosemary, and Honey Balsamic Drizzle

Creamed Rice with Cranberry Soup and Cardamom Whipped Cream (Riisipuuro)

Pink Grapefruit Brûlée with Tarragon Lime Sugar

Strawberry Cardamom Cream Cheese Crepes

Please don't let crepes scare you. They really aren't any harder to make than pancakes once you get the hang of it. A crepe pan definitely helps, but any lightweight, shallow skillet should work. For this recipe I've paired sweetened whipped cream cheese with a strawberry and cardamom–flavored chutney, but the filling options are almost endless, so if you do decide to invest in a crepe pan, you'll get plenty of use out of it. You can also use it to make small pancakes.

Makes 8 crepes.

Crepes

2 eggs, room temperature
3/4 cup whole milk, room temperature
1/2 cup water, room temperature
2 tablespoons butter, melted, plus more for crepe pan
1/2 teaspoon vanilla bean paste
2 teaspoons granulated sugar
1/2 teaspoon cardamom
1/8 teaspoon kosher salt
3/4 cup all-purpose flour
Powdered sugar, for dusting

Strawberry Chutney

1 cup strawberries, plus more for garnish
1 tablespoon granulated sugar
1 teaspoon vanilla bean paste
1 teaspoon cardamom

Whipped Cream Cheese

1 (8-ounce) package cream cheese, room temperature
2 tablespoons whole milk
1 tablespoon granulated sugar
1/2 teaspoon vanilla bean paste

For the Crepes

In a medium bowl whisk the eggs. Add the milk, water, melted butter, and vanilla bean paste and whisk to combine. Whisk in the granulated sugar, cardamom, and salt, then slowly add the flour, stirring to combine. Whisk until smooth and no lumps remain.

Cover the bowl with plastic wrap and refrigerate for at least 30 minutes and up to overnight. The chilling and resting allows any air bubbles to burst, the gluten to relax, and the flour to absorb the liquid, resulting in smoother, more tender crepes.

For the Chutney

In a small bowl mash the strawberries, sugar, vanilla bean paste, and cardamom with a fork or pastry blender until chunky.

For the Cream Cheese

In the bowl of a stand mixer fitted with the paddle attachment, beat the cream cheese, milk, sugar, and vanilla bean paste on medium speed for about 2 minutes until light and fluffy. (Alternatively, you can use a hand mixer.)

recipe continues

continued from page 215

To Assemble the Crepes

Heat a crepe pan or shallow 9-inch skillet over medium heat. Stir the batter to remix. Using a pastry brush, brush the pan with room temperature or melted butter. Ladle or pour in 1/4 cup batter, quickly tilting the pan so the batter spreads out evenly across the bottom. Cook the crepe until the edges start to brown and the center is set, about 1 minute. Flip the crepe using your fingers or a spatula and cook the other side for 10 to 15 seconds more.

Slide the crepe onto a wire rack and cover with a clean kitchen towel while you make the remaining seven crepes, repeating the above steps, lightly brushing the pan with butter between each crepe.

Spoon some of the whipped cream cheese and strawberry chutney onto half of each crepe, then fold in half and in half again to make a triangle. Garnish with additional whole strawberries and powdered sugar.

Tips for Perfect Crepes

Troubleshooting

The perfect crepe awaits, but just in case something goes wrong, here are some tips for fixing common crepe-making errors.

Bubbles in batter: overbeaten batter. Mix on a lower speed, and let the batter stand for a bit longer.

Lacy pattern around edges: batter too thin. This is common with the first crepe in the batch. Add a tablespoon or two of flour.

Batter won't spread evenly: batter too thick. Add a tablespoon of water or milk.

Batter sticks to pan: pan not hot enough or not enough butter in the pan.

Edges crack: batter too thin and pan too hot. Add some flour and turn down heat.

Holes in crepes: not enough batter in the pan. Use a bigger scoop.

Batter curdles in pan: too much butter in the pan.

Ways to Fold Crepes

There are almost as many ways to fold a crepe as there are ways to fill one. Here are a few suggestions.

Folded: Spread filling down the middle. Fold one side in and then the other.

Eggroll/burrito: Spread filling in center. Fold opposite sides in, then roll up the crepe.

Blintz/pocket: Spread filling in center. Fold two opposite sides in so they overlap a bit, then fold over the two remaining sides to make a pocket. Set fold down on the plate.

Cigar: Spread filling over entire crepe, then roll up jelly-roll style.

Half fold: Spread filling over entire crepe, then fold in half.

Crepe Suzette: Spread filling over entire crepe. Fold in half and then in half again to make a triangle.

Pyramid/triangle: Spread filling over entire crepe, fold in half, then fold over the top edge about a quarter of the way down. Repeat two more times to make a pyramid.

Cone: Spread filling over top half of crepe. Fold the bottom over toward the middle, then fold two sides in at an angle to make a cone. Tuck the top side underneath crepe.

Galette: Spread filling in center. Fold over the four sides toward the middle, leaving the center uncovered.

Appetizers: After rolling the crepe into a cigar or tube, cut into 1-inch or 2-inch sections.

Crepe cake: Stack flat crepes on top of each other, then cut into wedges to serve.

One-Bowl Strawberry Scones with Almond Drizzle

As anyone with chickens knows, hens stop (or drastically slow down) laying at various times of the year, so it's a good idea to have a few dessert recipes in your arsenal that don't require any eggs. These strawberry scones fit the bill. They come together quickly in one bowl and are always a hit. Choosing strawberries at the height of their freshness will result in sweeter scones.

Makes 8 scones.

- 2 1/2 cups all-purpose flour
- 3 tablespoons granulated sugar, plus more for sprinkling
- 1 tablespoon baking powder
- 1/4 teaspoon salt
- 1/2 cup (1 stick) butter, cold, cut into small pieces
- 1 cup sliced or diced fresh strawberries, plus whole berries for serving
- 1/2 cup plus 1 tablespoon heavy cream, divided
- 1 teaspoon vanilla bean paste
- 1/2 cup powdered sugar
- 2 tablespoons whole milk
- 1/4 teaspoon almond extract
- Honey butter or strawberry jam, for serving

Preheat the oven to 400 degrees. Line a rimmed baking sheet with parchment paper.

In a large bowl, mix the flour, sugar, baking powder, and salt. Use a pastry cutter or fork to incorporate the cold butter. Mix until the dough is clumpy, but it's okay if there are still some lumps of butter. Gently fold in the sliced strawberries. Mix 1/2 cup of the heavy cream and vanilla bean paste into the dough until just moistened.

Transfer the dough to a clean surface. Gently work the dough, just until the flour is incorporated. Move the ball of dough to the prepared baking sheet.

Pat the dough into an 8-inch circle about 3/4-inch thick. Use a sharp knife to cut the circle into eight wedges. Move the wedges slightly apart from each other, leaving them in a circle formation. Brush the tops with the remaining 1 tablespoon heavy cream and sprinkle with sugar.

Bake for 17 to 18 minutes or until the scones are light golden on top.

Let them cool slightly on the sheet, then place the scones on a wire rack set on top of the baking sheet to cool completely.

To make the almond drizzle, whisk the powdered sugar with the milk and almond extract. Then drizzle over the cooled scones.

Serve with whole strawberries, honey butter, or strawberry jam. Or all three.

Fresh Tip: Peek under the green "cap" of each strawberry to be sure you see red and not white. Fully ripe berries will be red from bottom to top.

Glazed Cardamom Peach Quick Bread

I feel like everyone needs an easy quick-bread recipe they can grab at a moment's notice and turn out a delicious loaf. This is mine. This simple recipe comes together in no time and really highlights the flavors of fresh summer peaches. If you don't like peaches, feel free to substitute any type of stone fruit or even berries.

Makes 1 loaf.

Butter for greasing the pan
2 cups diced fresh peaches (about 2 medium)
1/4 cup packed brown sugar
1/2 teaspoon ground cardamom
2 cups all-purpose flour
2 teaspoons baking powder
1/4 teaspoon kosher salt
1/2 cup butter, melted and cooled slightly
3/4 cup granulated sugar
2 eggs, room temperature
1/2 cup milk, room temperature
1 teaspoon almond extract, divided
1 teaspoon vanilla bean paste
1 cup powdered sugar

Preheat the oven to 350 degrees. Grease an 8 x 4-inch loaf pan and line with parchment, leaving two long ends hanging over the sides.

In a medium bowl combine the peaches, brown sugar, and cardamom. In a second medium bowl, whisk the flour, baking powder, and salt.

In a large mixing bowl, whisk the butter and granulated sugar. Add the eggs, one at a time, whisking between each addition, then add the milk and 1/2 teaspoon of the almond extract. Slowly add the flour mixture to the batter, whisking until just combined and scraping down the sides of the bowl as needed.

Pour half the batter into the prepared loaf pan. Spoon half of the fruit mixture on top, and cover with the remaining batter. Spoon the remaining fruit on top, reserving any juices for the glaze.

Bake for 60 to 65 minutes until golden brown on top and a toothpick inserted in the center comes out clean. Cover with foil if the top is browning too quickly. Cool in the pan on a wire rack for 10 minutes, then remove from the pan and cool completely on the rack.

While the loaf is cooling, in a small bowl whisk the reserved peach juices (about 2 tablespoons), powdered sugar, and the remaining 1/2 teaspoon almond extract until smooth.

Once the bread has cooled completely, drizzle with the frosting. Slice and serve.

½ TEASPOON

IN SEASON — SUMMER

Grilled Apricot and Burrata Caprese with Honey and Herb Oil

I love a good traditional tomato-mozzarella caprese salad but only when tomatoes are in season and are beautifully sun-ripened. It's just not worth the effort to make one with mediocre tomatoes. So during the off-season, when I'm craving a similar dish, I'll often sub in peaches—or in this case, grilled apricots—and lots of fresh herbs. I've used both fresh mozzarella and burrata in this recipe at different times, and both work equally well, so feel free to use whichever you would like. My apologies to the classic recipe, but to be fair, *caprese* merely means "from Capri," and Italy is one of the largest exporters of apricots—so I stand by my variation and am still calling it "caprese."

Makes 4 servings.

1 tablespoon olive oil, plus more for the grill
2 apricots, halved, pitted, and sliced into 8 wedges each
1 (8-ounce) burrata cheese ball, cut in half and then ripped or cut into chunks (or fresh mozzarella, thinly sliced)
12 fresh basil leaves, divided
12 fresh mint leaves, divided
12 fresh tarragon leaves, divided
Kosher salt
Freshly ground black pepper
1 tablespoon honey
1/2 teaspoon champagne vinegar

Brush a grill or grill pan with olive oil. Grill the apricot wedges until they are slightly softened but not falling apart and there are nice grill marks on both sides, about 2 minutes per side.

On a serving platter or plate, alternate the burrata and apricot slices, then tuck in eight each of the basil, mint, and tarragon leaves. Season with just a dash of salt and a few grinds of pepper.

In a small bowl whisk the honey and vinegar, then drizzle over the salad.

In a food processor or coffee grinder, puree the remaining basil, mint, and tarragon leaves with 1 tablespoon olive oil. Use a fine-mesh strainer to strain the liquid into a small bowl, then dot the plate with the herb oil.

Maine Wild Blueberry Pie

This is hands-down the very best blueberry pie you will ever eat. It's my father-in-law's secret family recipe. The "secret" is an impossibly flaky crust thanks to a capful of cider vinegar (vodka or white vinegar also works!) and Maine wild blueberries for the filling. Smaller than the high bush variety you normally see, Maine wild blueberries are sweeter and are packed with concentrated flavor, so they're perfect for pie. If you're not lucky enough to live in Maine and have access to fresh blueberries, you should be able to find Maine wild blueberries in the freezer section of your grocery store. You use them the same way you would use the fresh berries.

Makes 1 pie.

Pie Crust

2 1/2 cups all-purpose flour
1 teaspoon salt
1 teaspoon granulated sugar
1 cup (2 sticks) butter, cut into cubes and chilled
2 teaspoons cider vinegar, vodka, or white vinegar
1/4 to 1/2 cup ice water

Blueberry Filling

2 pints Maine wild blueberries, fresh or frozen (about 4 cups)
1/3 cup granulated sugar
1/3 cup firmly packed light brown sugar
1/4 cup cornstarch
1 tablespoon all-purpose flour
1/2 teaspoon cardamom (or substitute cinnamon if you want)
1 teaspoon lemon zest (about 1/3 lemon)
1 tablespoon freshly squeezed lemon juice (about 1/2 lemon)

To Assemble the Pie

1 egg, lightly whisked
1 tablespoon whole milk
1 tablespoon all-purpose flour
1 teaspoon granulated sugar
Vanilla ice cream, for serving (optional)

For the Crust

In the bowl of a food processor, combine the flour, salt, and sugar. Add the butter and pulse until the mixture resembles wet sand, about 15 or 20 times.

recipe continues

continued from page 225

While pulsing continuously, slowly add the cider vinegar and 1/4 cup of the ice water through the tube, just until the dough starts to form a ball, about 30 seconds. If the dough doesn't hold together when you pinch it between your fingers, add more ice water, a little at a time, stopping before the dough gets too sticky or looks wet. (Alternatively, cut the butter into the flour with a pastry cutter, then slowly add the water to the dough and knead.)

Divide the dough into two equal pieces. Flatten each into a disc and wrap in plastic wrap. Chill for at least 1 hour.

For the Filling

With a wooden spoon or spatula, gently mix the blueberries, granulated sugar, brown sugar, cornstarch, flour, cardamom, lemon zest, and lemon juice in a large mixing bowl.

Preheat the oven to 400 degrees and position the oven rack in the bottom third of the oven.

Whisk the egg and milk in a small bowl to make an egg wash.

Roll out the bottom crust on a floured surface and fit into a 9-inch pie plate. Sprinkle the flour over the crust. Pour the filling into the pie plate. Roll out the top crust on the floured surface and cut into 1/2-inch-wide strips with a pastry wheel, pizza cutter, or sharp knife. Weave the strips into a lattice top for the pie, trimming and crimping the edges. Brush the crust with the egg wash, then sprinkle with the sugar.

Cover the edges of the crust with foil and bake the pie for 15 minutes. Reduce the heat to 350 degrees, remove the foil, and continue to bake for 45 to 50 minutes, until the filling is bubbly and the crust is golden brown. If the crust is browning too quickly, re-cover with the foil.

Let the pie cool completely to set, at least several hours, then serve with ice cream, if desired. Refrigerate leftover pie.

Fresh Tip: Just like eggs, blueberries have a "bloom" on their surface that protects them from moisture loss and keeps them fresh. Unlike the bloom on eggs, which is usually invisible, the bloom on blueberries is a visible powdery white coating. Choosing berries with the bloom instead of glossy berries ensures that you're getting berries that have been picked at the height of freshness and have been protected from insects and the sun.

Pretty in Pink Raspberry Party Cupcakes

Extra egg whites make these cupcakes especially light and airy, while raspberry jam naturally tints the decadent Swiss meringue buttercream frosting a pretty pink color. These beauties would make a lovely addition to a little girl's birthday party, engagement party, baby shower, or Mother's Day luncheon.

Makes 12 cupcakes.

Raspberry Cupcakes

1 1/2 cups all-purpose flour
1 teaspoon baking powder
1/4 teaspoon baking soda
1/4 teaspoon kosher salt
1 tablespoon freshly squeezed lemon juice (about 1/2 lemon)
1/2 cup whole milk
1/2 cup (1 stick) butter, room temperature
3/4 cup granulated sugar
1 egg, plus 2 egg whites
1 teaspoon vanilla bean paste
1/2 cup seedless raspberry jam

Frosting

4 egg whites
1 cup superfine granulated sugar
1 1/2 cups (3 sticks) butter, cut into 1/2-inch cubes, room temperature
Pinch kosher salt
2 tablespoons seedless raspberry jam
Pink and white nonpareils for decoration (optional)

For the Cupcakes

Preheat the oven to 350 degrees. Line a 12-count cupcake pan with paper liners.

Whisk or stir the flour, baking powder, baking soda, and salt in a small bowl. In a liquid measuring cup, stir the lemon juice into the milk.

In the bowl of a stand mixer fitted with the paddle attachment, whip the butter and sugar on medium speed until fluffy and pale yellow, about 2 minutes. Add the whole egg, egg whites, and vanilla bean paste, and beat until combined. Reduce the mixer speed to low and add one third of the milk and lemon mixture, followed by one third of the flour mixture, alternating between them, until all the wet and dry mixtures are incorporated in the batter. Scrape down the sides of the mixing bowl with a rubber spatula as needed.

Using a 2-inch disher-style ice-cream or cookie scoop, divide the batter between the cups. Bake for about 18 to 20 minutes, or until the tops are light golden brown and a toothpick inserted into the center comes out clean. Remove from the oven, let cool for several minutes, then remove to a wire rack to cool completely.

recipe continues

continued from page 227

Once the cupcakes are cool, use a teaspoon or melon baller to scoop out a bit of the center of each cupcake. Spoon about 2 teaspoons of the jam into each. Alternatively, pipe some jam into the center of each cupcake using a pastry bag fitted with a large round piping tip.

For the Frosting

Bring a small saucepan of water to a simmer over medium heat. In the bowl of a stand mixer set over the saucepan, whisk the egg whites and sugar by hand (being careful not to let the bottom of the bowl touch the water). Using a candy thermometer to monitor the temperature, heat the mixture to 160 to 165 degrees, whisking occasionally. To test the mixture's consistency, rub a little between your fingers. When it's no longer gritty, set the bowl on the stand mixer fitted with the whisk attachment and beat on high speed for about 8 to 10 minutes, until stiff peaks form and the bowl is no longer warm.

Switch to the paddle attachment and add the butter a few cubes at a time, beating well to incorporate before adding more. Reduce the mixer speed to low, add the salt and jam, and beat for 2 to 3 minutes until the frosting is fluffy and smooth, scraping down the sides of the bowl as needed. Use a pastry bag fitted with a large round piping tip to frost the cupcakes, then garnish with the nonpareils, if desired.

Mixed Berry Brown Sugar Crumble

I can't think of a better way to enjoy fresh berries than in a baked crumble. I'm using both granulated and brown sugar to make the sweet crumble topping for these single-serving mixed berry crumbles in cocottes. You can use whatever type of berries you have or mix a few different kinds, which is my favorite way to enjoy this summer dessert.

Makes 6 servings.

6 cups fresh berries (a mixture of diced strawberries, blueberries, blackberries, and raspberries)
1/3 to 1/2 cup granulated sugar, adjusted depending on how sweet your berries are
2 teaspoons freshly squeezed lime juice (about 1/2 lime)
1 cup plus 2 tablespoons all-purpose flour, divided
1/2 cup (1 stick) butter, chilled, cut into cubes
1/2 cup firmly packed light brown sugar
Vanilla ice cream, for serving (optional)

Preheat the oven to 350 degrees.

In a large bowl mix the berries, granulated sugar, lime juice, and 2 tablespoons of the flour. Let sit while you make the topping.

Using a fork, mash the butter into the remaining 1 cup flour and the brown sugar. The flour should be mixed in, but your topping mixture should be crumbly, with small chunks of butter throughout. Divide the berries between six 8-ounce cocottes or oven-safe ramekins. Sprinkle the topping over the berries. Set the cocottes on a rimmed baking sheet and bake until golden brown on top and the filling is thick and bubbly, about 25 to 30 minutes.

Remove from the oven and let cool slightly. Serve with a scoop of vanilla ice cream, if desired. Refrigerate leftovers.

Roasted Grapes with Walnuts, Feta, Rosemary, and Honey Balsamic Drizzle

Roasting grapes brings out a wonderful sticky sweetness that is amplified by the honey balsamic drizzle. The feta cuts the sweetness and adds salt, while the roasted rosemary adds an earthy, herbaceous flavor. These roasted grapes make a nice addition to a cheese plate or charcuterie board and can be served with crackers or grilled bread.

Makes about 1 cup.

3/4 pound black seedless grapes
3 sprigs fresh rosemary leaves, plus more sprigs for garnish
1 tablespoon olive oil
1/2 teaspoon kosher salt
1/8 teaspoon freshly ground black pepper
1/4 cup balsamic vinegar
2 tablespoons honey
1 ounce feta, crumbled
2 tablespoons roasted walnut pieces

Preheat the oven to 375 degrees.

In a medium bowl toss the grapes and rosemary leaves with the olive oil, salt, and pepper, coating evenly. Spread evenly on a rimmed baking sheet. Roast for about 35 minutes, checking and stirring the grapes occasionally. When the grapes have softened and begin to burst and lose juice, remove them from the oven.

Meanwhile, in a small saucepan, simmer the balsamic vinegar and honey over low heat, whisking occasionally, until slightly reduced, about 5 minutes. The sauce will thicken as it cools.

To assemble the dish, spoon the grapes into a small bowl, add the feta, and season with salt. Pour the balsamic glaze over the grapes, and garnish with roasted walnut pieces and additional fresh rosemary.

Creamed Rice with Cranberry Soup and Cardamom Whipped Cream

(Riisipuuro)

Much of my love for old family recipes came from the year we lived in Finland when I was twelve years old. We stayed with my dad's relatives for a few weeks, and my favorite memory of that time (other than the indoor pool they had in their basement!) was the creamed rice (riisipuuro) my aunt served. I've dreamed of that dish for decades, so I knew I needed to re-create the recipe to include in this cookbook. Imagine a sweet risotto or rice pudding in a pool of cranberry sauce, topped with cardamom-scented whipped cream, and you have this fairly traditional Finnish dessert. Often served at Christmastime, an almond can be hidden in the rice, which is said to bring luck in the coming year to the person who finds it.

Makes 3 to 4 servings.

Creamed Rice

1 cup short-grain rice, such as Arborio or sushi rice
2 3/4 cups whole milk
1 1/4 cups heavy cream, divided
3 tablespoons granulated sugar, divided
2 teaspoons vanilla bean paste
1/4 teaspoon salt
1/4 teaspoon ground cardamom, for garnish

Cranberry Soup

1 cup cranberry juice
1/4 cup sugar
1 cup plus 2 tablespoons water, divided
2 tablespoons cornstarch

For the Rice

Combine the rice, milk, 1/4 cup of the cream, 2 tablespoons of the sugar, vanilla bean paste, and salt in a large saucepan. Bring to a low simmer, then continue to simmer, covered, over very low heat, stirring occasionally, until the liquid is absorbed and the rice is tender and creamy, about 40 minutes. Remove the rice to a large mixing bowl and cool for 20 minutes.

In the bowl of a stand mixer fitted with the whisk attachment, beat the remaining 1 cup cream to stiff peaks. Fold half of the whipped cream into the partially cooled rice.

Whisk the remaining 2 tablespoons sugar with the cardamom in a small bowl.

recipe continues

continued from page 235

For the Cranberry Soup

In a medium saucepan heat the cranberry juice, sugar, and 1 cup of the water to a boil. Whisk the cornstarch into the remaining 2 tablespoons water and slowly pour it into the boiling liquid. Bring back to a boil, then reduce the heat and continue to cook over medium heat until slightly thickened, about 6 to 8 minutes. Remove from the heat and cool to room temperature.

To Assemble

Spoon the rice into serving bowls. Ladle some of the fruit soup around the rice, then top with the reserved whipped cream. Sprinkle with the cardamom sugar. Serve with extra fruit soup in a pitcher tableside for pouring.

Pink Grapefruit Brûlée with Tarragon Lime Sugar

Here's another use for that kitchen torch you bought just to make crème brûlée. These brûléed grapefruit are an easy, elegant way to serve a bit of vitamin C for breakfast. And they are perfect for a holiday brunch. If you don't have a torch, you can pop the grapefruit halves on a rimmed baking sheet and broil them for 6 to 8 minutes until they're caramelized and amber in color.

Makes 2 servings.

1 pink grapefruit, halved
2 tablespoons granulated sugar, divided
Tarragon Lime Sugar, for sprinkling (recipe on page 239)
Fresh tarragon, for garnish

Trim the bottom of each grapefruit half so it sits level and won't tip over. With a small paring knife, cut around the inner edge of the pith and between each segment. Remove any seeds. Place the cut sides down on a folded paper towel and let sit for at least 5 minutes to remove any excess liquid. Then pat very dry.

Sprinkle 1 tablespoon of granulated sugar on one of the halves. Then, using the kitchen torch, melt the sugar until it's bubbling and light brown. Repeat with the other half. Set each half on a small plate and let cool for a bit to allow the sugar to harden. Sprinkle with some of the Tarragon Lime Sugar and garnish with fresh tarragon.

Tarragon Lime Sugar

I love this zesty Tarragon Lime Sugar with savory herbal notes. You can sprinkle it on angel food or pound cake, pancakes, or French toast. You can also substitute it for the sweetener in your favorite sugar cookie or cupcake recipe, or use it to rim cocktail glasses or stir into iced tea or lemonade. Here I'm using it to further sweeten the brûléed grapefruit halves. Inspired by Thalia Ho's recipe from her cookbook *Wild Sweetness* and Martha Stewart's *Everyday Food* from 2012, I've subbed in tarragon for the basil and lime zest for the lemon in the original recipes—and added a pinch of salt to bring out the other flavors.

Makes about 1/4 cup.

1/4 cup granulated sugar
1 tablespoon fresh tarragon leaves
1/4 teaspoon lime zest (less than 1/2 lime)
Pinch of kosher salt

Using a coffee grinder or food processor, pulse the sugar, tarragon, lime zest, and salt until just combined, about 20 seconds.

Leftovers can be refrigerated or stored in an airtight container at room temperature and should be used within 1 month.

CUSTARD AND PUDDING

Fresh Tip: Eggs separate more easily when they're cold, but they whip up better at room temperature—so take your eggs out of the refrigerator and separate them, then let them come to room temperature while you measure out the rest of your ingredients before whipping them.

Warm Molten Lemon Soufflé Cakes

These individual serving-size cakes deliver two different textures in each creamy bite. The bottom is luscious, jammy lemon curd, while the top is fluffy and soufflé-like. But be sure not to overcook them, or the bottoms won't be molten. Dollop some whipped cream on top for more decadence!

Makes 6.

3 lemons, divided
3 eggs, separated, room temperature
1 cup whole milk, room temperature
1/4 cup all-purpose flour
1/8 teaspoon kosher salt
1 cup granulated sugar, divided
Powdered sugar, for dusting
Whipped cream, for serving (optional)

Preheat the oven to 350 degrees. Heat a kettle of water on the stove. Set six ungreased 6-ounce oven-safe ramekins into a 9 x 13-inch baking pan.

Zest and juice 1 lemon, then juice a second lemon. Cut the third lemon into thin slices and reserve for garnish. Whisk the egg yolks, milk, lemon juice, and zest in a medium mixing bowl. Add the flour, salt, and all but 1 tablespoon of the granulated sugar, and whisk until smooth.

With a hand mixer, or in the bowl of a stand mixer fitted with the whisk attachment, beat the egg whites for about 30 seconds on high until frothy, then sprinkle the reserved tablespoon of granulated sugar on top and continue to beat to stiff, glossy peaks, about 1 minute longer.

Gently fold the beaten egg whites into the milk mixture, in thirds, until all the lumps are gone. Divide the batter among the ramekins, filling them almost all the way to the top. Pour 1 inch of the hot water into the casserole dish, then carefully set it in the oven on the middle rack.

Bake until puffy, light golden brown on top, and starting to pull away from the edges of the ramekins, about 30 to 35 minutes. Carefully remove the ramekins from the water bath to a wire rack to cool for 15 minutes.

Dust with powdered sugar and garnish each with a lemon slice and scoop of whipped cream, if desired. Cover and refrigerate leftovers for up to 3 days.

Lemon Butter Cookies with Lemon Curd Filling

These adorable egg-shaped cookies filled with zesty lemon curd are my spirit cookies! They're the perfect blend of tart and sweet and of course look like little eggs. If you don't have an egg-shaped cookie cutter, you can use a 2-inch round cookie cutter instead. Either way, use the wide end of a large piping tip to cut the 1-inch circles in the tops of the cookies to let the bright yellow curd poke through.

Makes 12 sandwich cookies.

Lemon Curd

Makes about 1 1/4 cups.

3 eggs
3/4 cup sugar
1/4 cup fresh squeezed citrus juice
1/2 stick butter, room temperature, cut into 1/2-inch cubes

Cookies

1/2 cup (1 stick) butter, room temperature
1/2 cup granulated sugar
1/4 teaspoon kosher salt
1 egg yolk
1 tablespoon heavy cream
1 tablespoon lemon zest (about 1 lemon)
2 tablespoons lemon juice (about 1 lemon)
1 3/4 cups all-purpose flour
Powdered sugar, for dusting

For the Lemon Curd

Set a medium heat-proof glass or stainless steel bowl over a saucepan of simmering water (being careful not to let the bowl touch the water). Whisk the eggs and sugar in the bowl until smooth. Then add the citrus juice and whisk to combine.

Continue to cook, whisking for several minutes, until the mixture is warmed through. Then add the butter, a few cubes at a time, whisking in between each addition until the butter melts completely.

Once all the butter is incorporated, continue to whisk, cooking until the curd thickens slightly and coats the back of a spoon, about 20 to 25 minutes.

If you have a candy thermometer, heat the curd to between 180 and 185 degrees.

Once the curd has thickened to the correct consistency, remove the bowl from the heat, and strain the curd through a fine-mesh strainer into a small bowl. Let cool to room temperature and refrigerate.

recipe continues

continued from page 245

For the Cookies

Preheat the oven to 350 degrees. Line two rimmed baking sheets with parchment paper.

With a hand mixer or in the bowl of a stand mixer fitted with the paddle attachment, beat the butter until light and creamy, then add the sugar and salt and beat until smooth and combined. Beat in the egg yolk, then add the heavy cream, lemon zest, and juice. Mix until combined, scraping down the sides with a rubber spatula if necessary. On low speed, mix in the flour until just combined.

Divide the dough into two disks, wrap in plastic wrap, and chill for 30 minutes.

On a lightly floured surface, roll out one of the discs to 1/8-inch thick and cut into 12 egg shapes or circles. Repeat with the second disc of dough, but also cut one a 1-inch circular cutout in each of the second batch of cookies. Reroll the trimmings and repeat until you have 24 cookies total. Place the cookies on the prepared baking sheets 1/2 inch apart.

Bake the cookies for 8 to 9 minutes or until the edges are just barely browned. Let cool for 5 minutes, then slide the parchment onto a wire rack to allow the cookies to cool completely.

To Assemble the Sandwich Cookies

Once the cookies are cooled, spread a teaspoon of the lemon curd onto each of the 12 whole cookie bases. Sift powdered sugar over the 12 cutout cookie tops, then, carefully holding each cookie top by the edges, place one on top of each lemon curd cookie base.

Store the cookies in the refrigerator for up to a week.

Fresh Tip: Lemons with the smoothest skin will yield the most juice. And be sure to roll the lemon on the counter a few times before cutting it in half. That will yield more juice as well.

Maple Brown Sugar Pots de Crème with Bourbon Whipped Cream

Pot de crème is a traditional French dessert whose name literally means "pot of cream." While chocolate is a common flavoring, I decided to give them a more New England feel. When you're craving the coziness of fall on a spring day during syrup tapping season, try these fall-inspired pots sweetened with maple syrup and brown sugar. They're baked in a water bath to ensure that they are silky and smooth, then topped with boozy whipped cream and salty-sweet praline bits.

Makes 4.

Pecan Praline Bacon Bits

4 slices regular-cut bacon
1/4 cup chopped pecans
3 tablespoons firmly packed brown sugar
1 tablespoon maple syrup

Bourbon Whipped Cream

1/2 cup heavy cream
2 teaspoons powdered sugar
1 tablespoon bourbon

Pots de Crème

1 cup heavy cream
1/2 cup whole milk
4 egg yolks
1/3 cup maple syrup
2 tablespoons firmly packed brown sugar
1 teaspoon vanilla bean paste
1/4 teaspoon kosher salt

For the Bacon Bits

Preheat the oven to 400 degrees. Line a rimmed baking sheet with foil and place a wire rack on top. Arrange the bacon strips in a single layer, and cook until very crispy and browned, about 22 to 23 minutes.

Meanwhile, combine the pecans and sugar in a small bowl. Brush the tops of the browned bacon strips with the maple syrup, then press the nut mixture evenly on top. Bake until the topping is crystallized and bubbly, about 7 to 8 minutes. Remove from the oven and cool completely on the rack, then chop into small pieces.

For the Whipped Cream

In the bowl of a stand mixer with the whisk attachment or using a hand mixer, beat the cream on high speed for 30 seconds until frothy. Add the sugar and bourbon and continue to beat until soft peaks form, about 90 seconds.

recipe continues

continued from page 247

For the Pots de Crème

Preheat the oven to 325 degrees. Bring a kettle of water to a boil.

In a medium saucepan simmer the heavy cream and milk over medium heat just until bubbles begin to form on the surface. Remove the pan from the heat.

Meanwhile, whisk the egg yolks, maple syrup, brown sugar, vanilla bean paste, and salt in a medium bowl until smooth and combined. Slowly ladle about half of the milk mixture to the egg mixture, one ladleful at a time, whisking to combine as you pour so the eggs don't curdle. Then pour the mixture back into the remaining milk mixture in the saucepan and whisk until fully incorporated. Pour through a fine-mesh strainer into a 2-cup measuring cup.

Set four 4-ounce ramekins or small oven-proof containers into a baking pan. Divide the custard among the ramekins. Place the pan in the oven, then add the hot water until it comes about halfway up the sides of the ramekins, about 1/2-inch deep.

Bake the custards until almost set—the centers will still be jiggly—about 35 minutes. Carefully remove the baking pan from the oven without splashing water into the ramekins. Place the ramekins on a wire rack until they are cool enough to touch, then remove them from the water bath and cool completely on the racks.

To serve the pots de crème, top with a dollop of Bourbon Whipped Cream, then sprinkle with the Pecan Praline Bacon Bits. Cover and refrigerate leftovers.

Honey Vanilla Yogurt Cups with Berries and Mint

I honestly eat eggs almost every morning for breakfast, but I sometimes enjoy a warm bowl of oatmeal in the winter with cardamom and cream, when the chickens aren't laying. Or sometimes as a treat, I'll enjoy these refreshing yogurt cups on a warm summer morning. They're healthier than sweetened, flavored yogurts you buy at the store since you can control the level of sweetness—and they're super easy to make. The bit of honey and candied ginger in the bottom of each glass is key—it's a sweet surprise at the end.

Makes 6 servings.

- 1 to 2 tablespoons honey, plus more for drizzling
- 3 pieces candied ginger, cut into small chunks (about 2 tablespoons)
- 1/2 teaspoon vanilla bean paste
- 24 ounces plain Greek yogurt (about 3 cups)
- 36 blueberries (about 1/2 cup)
- 12 blackberries (about 1 cup)
- 6 fresh mint sprigs

Drizzle a bit of honey in the bottom of six 4-ounce glasses or ramekins, then divide the ginger among the glasses.

In a medium bowl whisk 1 to 2 tablespoons of the honey and the vanilla bean paste into the yogurt. Spoon or pipe the yogurt into the glasses.

Top with the blueberries, blackberries, and fresh mint. Drizzle with more honey if desired.

Blackberry Basil Ice Cream

I love combining sweet and savory flavors in desserts, especially when it comes to herbs and berries. This combination might seem odd at first, but trust me, it's a winner! The key is steeping the fresh basil leaves in the milk as it's simmering to impart that bold, herbaceous flavor.

Makes about 2 quarts.

- 1 cup loosely packed fresh basil leaves, plus more for garnish
- 4 cups whole milk
- 2 cups heavy cream
- 2 teaspoons vanilla bean paste
- 4 egg yolks
- 1 1/4 cups granulated sugar
- 1/2 teaspoon kosher salt
- 1/2 cup chopped white chocolate or white chocolate chips (optional)
- 1/2 cup seedless blackberry jam

Chill your ice cream maker insert, as indicated in the manufacturer's instructions.

Tear the basil leaves or rub them between your fingers to release some of the oils. In a medium saucepan simmer the milk, cream, and basil over medium-high heat for several minutes, just until bubbles form around the edges. Remove the pan from heat, stir in the vanilla bean paste, and let the basil steep and the mixture cool for 10 minutes. Then strain into a large bowl and discard the basil.

In a medium bowl whisk the egg yolks, sugar, and salt. Slowly add a few ladlefuls of the warm milk mixture to the egg mixture, one ladleful at a time, whisking between each to prevent curdling. Then pour the egg mixture into the saucepan along with the remaining milk mixture.

Return the pan to the stove and cook over medium-low heat for 2 to 3 minutes, whisking constantly, to thoroughly warm the liquid. Remove the pan from the heat and pour the mixture into a large bowl. Use a rubber spatula to scrape the pan clean and make sure all the flecks of vanilla transfer to the bowl. Refrigerate the custard until cooled, at least 1 hour or overnight.

Once the custard is thoroughly chilled, pour it into your ice cream maker and follow the manufacturer's instructions, adding the chopped white chocolate during the last few minutes of churning, if using. Then transfer half of the mixture to a loaf pan or other freezer-safe container. Spread half of the jam on top, and use a butter knife to swirl the jam through the ice cream. Repeat with the remaining ice cream and jam. Then cover the pan with plastic wrap and freeze for several hours until it sets.

Scoop the ice cream into bowls and garnish with fresh basil leaves.

Fresh Tip: If you have a basil plant on your windowsill, note that basil prefers to be watered from the bottom, so keep the base of the container submerged in water for the longevity of the plant, and don't water from the top directly into the soil.

Pistachio Pudding

Homemade pistachio pudding is nothing like pudding from a box. It's way better, of course, and it's not neon green. It's actually going to turn out a nice earthy, pale green color, but if you want a more pronounced green, a bit of blue (yes, blue!) food coloring will turn it a beautiful, sublime greenish color. I use plant-based spirulina food coloring from Color Kitchen Foods, but feel free to omit it if you wish or use regular food coloring. This pudding is super easy to make and has a delicious, natural, earthy pistachio flavor. Eat it right from the bowl, or use it to fill tarts, éclairs, or cream puffs.

Makes about 2 cups (4 servings).

Pistachio Pudding

1 cup shelled dry-roasted unsalted pistachios, plus more for garnish
1 cup granulated sugar, divided
2 cups whole milk, divided
3 egg yolks
2 tablespoons cornstarch
1/8 teaspoon kosher salt
2 tablespoons butter
1/4 to 1/2 teaspoon spirulina powder or a few drops of blue food coloring, if desired

Whipped Cream

1 cup heavy cream
2 teaspoons sugar
Pinch kosher salt

For the Pistachio Pudding

In a food processor or blender, pulse the pistachios until they are finely ground. Then add 1/2 cup of the sugar and 1/2 cup of the milk and continue to process until the mixture is smooth and forms a paste, scraping down the sides of the bowl as needed, about 5 minutes. In a medium bowl whisk the egg yolks, the remaining 1/2 cup sugar, cornstarch, and salt until combined.

In a medium saucepan whisk the pistachio paste into the remaining 1 1/2 cups milk over medium heat, just until the edges start to bubble. Remove the pan from the heat and spoon a few ladlefuls of the hot milk mixture into the egg mixture, one at a time, whisking vigorously between ladlefuls to temper the egg yolks so they won't curdle.

Pour the egg mixture into the pot and continue to cook over low heat for 3 to 4 minutes, stirring or whisking until the mixture is bubbly and thick. Remove from the heat and whisk in the butter until it melts and is completely incorporated. Press the pudding through a fine-mesh strainer into a medium bowl. Stir in the food coloring, if using, until you reach the desired pale green tint, there are no streaks, and the color is uniform.

recipe continues

continued from page 255

Divide the pudding into four dessert cups or ramekins and press plastic wrap onto the surface to prevent a skin from forming on the top. Refrigerate for at least 2 hours before serving to let the pudding continue to thicken and set up.

For the Whipped Cream

In the bowl of a stand mixer fitted with the whisk attachment or using a hand mixer, beat the cream, sugar, and salt until stiff peaks form.

When ready to serve, top each pudding with a dollop of whipped cream and some additional chopped pistachios.

Earl Grey Crème Brûlée

Steeping Earl Grey tea bags in the warm milk mixture before whisking in the eggs will give your crème brûlée a subtle citrus fragrance without taking away from the simplicity of this classic dessert. Although I normally add vanilla to my crème brûlée, the only flavoring this recipe needs is the bergamot tea bags. I am generally a traditionalist when it comes to crème brûlée, but this is a subtle variation that I really enjoy making.

Makes 4.

5 egg yolks, whisked
2 cups heavy cream
1/3 cup granulated sugar
3 Earl Grey tea bags
1/8 teaspoon kosher salt
2 to 3 tablespoons superfine sugar
Whipped cream, for serving (optional)

Preheat the oven to 325 degrees. Place four 6-ounce shallow ramekins into a baking pan. Set a kettle of water on the stove to boil.

In a small bowl whisk the egg yolks until smooth. In a medium saucepan, combine the heavy cream and granulated sugar and simmer over medium-low heat, whisking until the sugar dissolves and bubbles just start to form on the surface. Remove the pan from the stove and add the tea bags. Let the tea steep for 15 minutes, then remove the tea bags, pressing gently on them to release some of the liquid. Slowly whisk the egg yolks and salt into the cream mixture until combined.

Strain the liquid through a fine-mesh strainer set over a 2-cup measuring cup, discarding the solids. Pour the strained liquid into the four 6-ounce ramekins, dividing the liquid evenly. Set the baking pan in the oven and carefully pour boiling water into the baking pan until it comes halfway up the sides of the ramekins, about 1/2-inch deep (this will prevent the custards from cracking and drying out).

Bake until the custard is just set and the centers still move slightly when gently shaken, about 25 to 30 minutes. Carefully remove the baking pan from the oven, being careful not to splash any water into the custard. Set the ramekins on a wire rack to cool to room temperature, at least an hour. Then cover them with plastic wrap and chill for at least 3 hours or up to 2 days.

recipe continues

continued from page 257

To serve, remove the ramekins from the refrigerator and evenly cover the top of each custard with about 2 teaspoons of superfine sugar, gently tipping and shaking each ramekin to be sure the top of the custard is completely covered.

Brown the tops with a handheld kitchen torch, moving it back and forth across the sugar until it melts and bubbles. Continue until the sugar becomes aromatic, turns a deep, rich caramel-brown color, and solidifies into a solid, smooth sheet. Let the custards sit for a minute, until the topping hardens, then serve immediately with a dollop of whipped cream, if desired.

Fresh Tip: If you don't have a kitchen torch, you can brown the tops another way. For each custard, you need 2 tablespoons of granulated or superfine sugar and 1 tablespoon of water. Heat the sugar and water over medium heat in a pan (a stainless steel or light-colored pan is best so you can see the sugar's color changing), stirring until the sugar dissolves. Once the sugar has dissolved, stop stirring. The sugar will quickly start to bubble, caramelize, and turn golden. At that point, it should be quickly poured over the chilled custard, tilting the ramekin to make a thin, even layer. Watch the sugar carefully because it can burn quickly.

Traditional New England Indian Pudding

Indian Pudding, which is sort of like a soft spiced gingerbread or custard, will never win an award in the looks department, but is an oddly delicious, comforting dish served warm, often under a scoop of vanilla ice cream. It's one of the first uniquely American recipes, likely adapted from British hasty pudding by early New England settlers with Native American cornmeal standing in for the traditional wheat flour. The cornmeal is baked slowly with molasses, brown sugar, vanilla, and spices until soft-set. It's the ultimate cozy dessert!

Makes 6 to 8 servings.

Butter and granulated sugar, for prepping the dish
4 cups whole milk
3 tablespoons butter
1/2 cup yellow cornmeal
1/2 cup molasses
1/2 cup firmly packed light brown sugar
1 teaspoon vanilla bean paste
1/2 teaspoon ground cinnamon
1/2 teaspoon ground ginger
1/8 teaspoon freshly grated nutmeg
1/2 teaspoon kosher salt
3 eggs, lightly whisked
Vanilla ice cream, for serving (optional)

Preheat the oven to 300 degrees. Grease and sugar an 8 x 8-inch baking dish or pie plate.

In a medium saucepan over medium-low heat, bring the milk and butter to a simmer. Stir in the cornmeal and cook, stirring occasionally, until the mixture is bubbling, smooth, and slightly thickened, about 10 minutes.

Remove from the heat and whisk in the molasses, sugar, vanilla bean paste, cinnamon, ginger, nutmeg, and salt until well combined. Pour the eggs into the pan in a slow drizzle, whisking to prevent the eggs from curdling. Scrape the batter into the prepared baking dish—it will be very runny.

Bake for 2 hours, until the edges are set and the top is glossy. It's okay if the middle is still a bit jiggly. Remove from the oven and allow to cool for about 30 minutes, then spoon into individual serving dishes and top with a scoop of vanilla ice cream. Refrigerate leftovers.

"Burnt" Basque Cheesecake

This definitely isn't your traditional New York cheesecake. But this recipe from the Basque region of Spain is super low maintenance since it requires no crust, no springform pan, and no water bath, and it just might become your favorite cheesecake to make! Baked at a high temperature until almost burned, this smooth, silky delicacy with a caramelized top needs no additional toppings or accompaniments. It's perfect just the way it is. I've taken the liberty of adding some hazelnut liqueur to the classic recipe, but you can omit it if you wish.

Makes one 9-inch cheesecake.

4 (8-ounce) packages cream cheese, room temperature
1 1/4 cups granulated sugar
1/2 teaspoon kosher salt
5 eggs, room temperature
3 tablespoons hazelnut liqueur (optional)
1 tablespoon vanilla bean paste
1 3/4 cups heavy cream, room temperature
3 tablespoons all-purpose flour

Preheat the oven to 425 degrees with the rack in the middle. Crumple up two sheets of parchment paper, then spread them flat and press them into a 9-inch springform pan or regular cake pan, making sure the paper comes all the way up the sides and over the top rim of the pan. Fold the extra paper down.

With a hand mixer or in the bowl of a stand mixer fitted with the paddle attachment, beat the cream cheese on low speed until very smooth and creamy, about 3 minutes, scraping down the sides of the bowl as needed. It's very important to beat the cream cheese until no lumps remain before adding the other ingredients, but keep the speed low to avoid beating in lots of air. Then add the sugar and salt and beat on low speed until smooth and well combined, about 2 minutes.

Add the eggs, one at a time, beating well between each addition and scraping down the sides of the bowl as needed. Add the hazelnut liqueur, if using, and vanilla bean paste. With the motor running, pour the heavy cream into the batter and beat until combined. Sift the flour through a fine-mesh strainer and mix just until the flour is incorporated.

recipe continues

continued from page 263

Pour the batter into the prepared pan, smooth the top, and bang the pan on the counter several times to remove any air bubbles.

Bake for about 45 minutes until the top is dark golden brown and looks almost burned and is puffy (the cheesecake will deflate as it cools). The middle should still be jiggly. If the top isn't as dark as you would like, switch the oven to broil and let the top darken up for a minute or two, but be sure to watch carefully—I leave the oven door open a crack so I can watch that it doesn't get too dark. You don't want to overbake the cheesecake.

Cool for at least 2 hours on a wire rack, then remove the sides of the springform pan (or carefully lift the cheesecake out of the cake pan using the parchment paper), and refrigerate, loosely covered. Chill for at least a few hours, preferably overnight.

To serve, let the cheesecake warm a bit to room temperature after removing from the refrigerator, then peel back the parchment paper and slice. Cover and refrigerate leftovers and eat within 3 or 4 days.

Fresh Tip: Use an instant-read thermometer to check the internal temperature. The cheesecake is done when the center registers 155 degrees.

Deep-Dish French Silk Chocolate Hazelnut Pie

This rich dessert is sure to delight the chocoholics in your family! A more elegant version of a chocolate cream pie, this recipe uses whipped eggs to create a silky-smooth filling, and I've added chocolate hazelnut spread for an additional layer of decadence. The recipe is easy to make but does require a fair amount of beating—and adequate time to set. It's great for summer entertaining because you make it the day before and then just finish it off with some whipped cream prior to serving. And if you want to make it a truly no-bake pie, you can use a prepared crust instead of making your own.

Makes one 9-inch pie.

Crust

1 1/4 cups all-purpose flour
1 teaspoon sugar
1/2 teaspoon kosher salt
1/2 cup (1 stick) butter, chilled, cut into cubes
1/4 cup ice water

Chocolate Hazelnut Filling

1/4 cup chocolate hazelnut spread
1 cup (2 sticks) butter, room temperature
1 cup granulated sugar
1/4 teaspoon kosher salt
4 ounces good-quality semisweet chocolate, melted and cooled until no longer warm but still liquid
2 teaspoons vanilla bean paste
4 eggs

Topping

3 cups heavy cream
4 tablespoons powdered sugar, sifted
2 teaspoons vanilla bean paste
Chocolate curls for garnish

For the Crust

In a food processor, pulse the flour, sugar, and salt to combine. Add the butter and pulse ten or twelve times to incorporate the butter into the dry ingredients. Continue to pulse, and slowly pour in the ice water just until the dough starts to hold together and form a ball.

Alternatively, cut the butter into the flour with a pastry cutter, then slowly add the water to the dough and knead.

recipe continues

continued from page 265

Wrap the dough in plastic wrap and flatten into a disk. Chill for 30 minutes.

Preheat the oven to 400 degrees. Roll out the dough on a floured surface and arrange in a deep-dish pie plate, crimping the edges. Prick the bottom with a fork and chill for another 30 minutes. Line the pan with parchment and fill with pie weights. Bake for 20 minutes, then remove the parchment and bake for another 10 to 15 minutes until light golden brown. Remove from the oven and cool completely.

For the Filling

Spread the chocolate hazelnut spread evenly over the cooled crust.

In the bowl of a stand mixer fitted with the paddle attachment or using a hand mixer, beat the butter, sugar, and salt on medium-high until light and fluffy, about 2 to 3 minutes. Add the melted chocolate and beat to combine. Then mix in the vanilla bean paste.

Scrape down the sides of the bowl and switch to the whisk attachment. Add one egg to the batter and beat on medium speed for 5 minutes. Then add the remaining eggs, one at a time, beating for 5 minutes between each addition and scraping down the sides of the bowl as needed. After adding the last egg and beating for 5 minutes, rub a bit of the filling between your fingers. It should feel smooth, not grainy. If you still feel any sugar granules, beat for another couple of minutes, until the filling is smooth and silky. It will be fairly loose but will firm up in the refrigerator. Scrape the filling into the crust. Smooth the top, cover with plastic wrap, and refrigerate the pie for at least 6 hours, preferably overnight, to let the filling thicken and set.

For the Topping

When ready to serve, with a hand mixer or in the clean bowl of a stand mixer fitted with the whisk attachment, beat the cream, sugar, and vanilla bean paste on medium-high speed until stiff peaks form, about 3 minutes.

Top the pie with the whipped cream and garnish with chocolate curls. Refrigerate leftovers.

Note: This recipe uses raw eggs. Anyone pregnant, nursing, or with a compromised immune system should take care eating raw or undercooked eggs due to the risk of salmonella. I recommend using only your own cleanest, freshest eggs for this recipe or use pasteurized eggs.

Portuguese Milk Tarts

(Queijadas de Leite)

Friends of ours recently vacationed in the Azores and brought us back the most delicious little custardy tarts dusted with copious amounts of powdered sugar. With nothing but the bakery bag they came in to go by, I did a little Googling and learned that they are called queijadas. They were so good—and since I don't have plans to travel overseas in the near future, I decided to create my own recipe. I tried a few recipes I found online, but they weren't quite right. Then I stumbled across a Portuguese site, translated the recipe, converted the grams to cups, and voilà! Perfection. I made them again, simplifying the recipe a bit and adding some lemon zest and nutmeg. Turns out, the tarts are extremely simple to make since they create their own crust. And who doesn't love that? This one's for you, Tyne and Kris! Thank you for the inspiration you brought back from your vacation.

Makes 24.

Butter and flour, for prepping the tins
2 cups whole milk
5 tablespoons butter, cubed
2 eggs
1 1/2 cups granulated sugar
1 cup all-purpose flour
1 teaspoon lemon zest (about 1/3 lemon)
1/8 teaspoon freshly grated nutmeg
Powdered sugar, for dusting

Preheat the oven to 350 degrees. Grease and flour two 12-count muffin tins.

In a medium saucepan over low heat, warm the milk and butter just until the butter melts. Set aside to cool slightly. In a medium bowl whisk the eggs, then whisk in the sugar. Add the flour and whisk until just combined, then slowly whisk in the milk mixture, lemon zest, and nutmeg until the batter is smooth. The batter will be very thin, like crepe or pancake batter. Don't overmix the batter or beat too much air into it. These tarts are supposed to be fairly flat.

Divide the batter between the muffin cups, filling each about halfway full. Bake for 20 to 22 minutes until crispy and golden around the edges but still soft in the middle. Cool for 10 to 15 minutes in the pan, then use a small spatula or knife to gently loosen them. Set the tarts on a wire rack to cool completely. The tarts will deflate as they cool.

Once cooled to room temperature, dust generously with powdered sugar and serve.

These are best eaten the day they're made, but you can store leftovers in an airtight container at room temperature for up to 2 days, or refrigerate them for longer storage. These should not be eaten hot. Wait until they're completely cooled and set to enjoy.

Fresh Tip: Pour the batter into a 2-cup measuring cup to easily (and neatly) fill each cup. Continue to refill the measuring cup from your mixing bowl as you divvy up the batter between the cups.

COCKTAILS AND BEVERAGES

Sydney Sunrise

Strawberry Basil Limeade

Blackberry Vanilla Shrub Cocktail

Vietnamese Egg Soda
(Soda Sữa Hột Gà)

Vietnamese Egg Coffee
(Cà Phê Trứng)

Honey Ginger Whiskey Sour

Barista-Style Cinnamon Latte

Mulled Spiced Wine
(Scandinavian Glögg)

White Christmas Cocktail

Sydney Sunrise

For a quick morning meal on the go, try this easy recipe for a "breakfast in a blender." Pour it over ice or blend some ice cubes into it to make a smoothie. It's the perfect way to start your morning—and is even said to be a cure for a hangover!

Makes 1 serving.

4 ounces orange juice (about 1/2 cup)
2 tablespoons freshly squeezed lime juice (about 1 lime)
1 egg
4 teaspoons honey
Orange slice, for garnish

Add the orange juice, lime juice, egg, and honey to a blender and blend until frothy and combined. Pour over ice in a glass and garnish with a slice of fresh orange.

***Note:** This recipe uses a raw egg. Anyone pregnant, nursing, or with a compromised immune system should take care eating raw or undercooked eggs due to the risk of salmonella. I recommend using only your own cleanest, freshest eggs for this recipe or use pasteurized eggs.*

Strawberry Basil Limeade

I love adding culinary herbs to sweet beverages to cut the sweetness a bit and add an unexpected savory depth of flavor. The strawberry and basil–infused simple syrup and fresh lime juice in this recipe turn a ho-hum glass of lemonade into a sweet sipper that's just bursting with summer flavors.

Makes 1 pitcher.

- 2 cups granulated sugar
- 2 cups water
- 2 cups strawberries, sliced in half, plus more for garnish
- 1/2 cup packed fresh basil leaves, ripped or torn, plus more for garnish
- Strips of rind from two limes
- 1 1/2 cups fresh lime juice, plus a few slices for garnish (about 12 limes)

To make the strawberry simple syrup, combine the sugar, water, strawberries, basil, and lime rind in a small saucepan and heat, stirring to dissolve the sugar. Simmer for several minutes, then turn off the heat and let sit until completely cooled. Strain and set aside.

In a large pitcher, combine 2 cups cold water, lime juice, and strawberry simple syrup to taste. Add additional halved strawberries and stir to mix well. Pour into glasses with ice and garnish with additional basil leaves, lime slices, and whole strawberries.

Fresh tip: Choose limes with the smoothest skins for the most juice. Also be sure the limes are room temperature, and then roll each lime against the counter, pressing down, before cutting in half, to help break up the fibers and release more juice.

Blackberry Vanilla Shrub Cocktail

If you've never had a shrub, you're in for a treat! Popular in colonial New England, shrubs are technically "drinking vinegar," syrupy liquid created by mixing equal parts vinegar (usually cider vinegar), fruit juices, and sugar—sort of like a vinegar-based simple syrup that was used to preserve fruits and berries. That fruit-infused vinegar is then added to sparkling water—or used as the base for various mixed drinks. I guess shrubs can be an acquired taste, but I love their fruity tartness. You owe it to yourself to try one—at least once. Plus, shrubs are a great way to use up berries that are slightly past their prime.

Makes 1 cocktail or mocktail.

Blackberry Vanilla Shrub

Makes about 1½ cups.

1 cup blackberries, plus more for garnish
1 cup granulated sugar
1 vanilla bean, split in half and the seeds scraped out
1 cup cider vinegar

Shrub Cocktail

1 ounce Blackberry Vanilla Shrub
1 ounce vodka, tequila, bourbon, or rum (optional)
5 ounces sparkling water, club soda, or ginger ale
Mint leaves, for garnish (optional)

For the Shrub

Put the blackberries, sugar, and vanilla bean and seeds in a quart mason jar, then mash them into a paste with a wooden spoon or fork. Pour the vinegar over the berries, stir well, or cover and shake, then refrigerate for at least 4 days (and up to several weeks) to allow the flavors to combine and deepen. Strain the liquid through a fine-mesh strainer, pressing down to release all the liquid, and discard the solids. If there are still small bits in the liquid, rinse out the strainer, line it with cheesecloth, and strain the liquid again.

Leftover shrub mixture can be stored in the refrigerator for several months.

For the Cocktail

Fill a glass with ice, then add the shrub mixture. Add 1 ounce of your preferred spirit to the glass, if desired.

Fill the glass with the club soda, ginger ale, or sparkling water. Garnish with blackberries and mint, if desired.

Fresh Tip: Look for raw apple cider vinegar with the "mother" for the best taste and health benefits. Cider vinegar is thought to help with digestion and control blood sugar levels and is a good source of probiotics and antioxidants.

Vietnamese Egg Soda

(Soda Sữa Hột Gà)

This cool carbonated beverage is a nice homemade substitution for a cream soda. A traditional Vietnamese drink, its name *soda sữa hột gà* literally translates to "soda, milk, egg yolk." The ingredients combine to form a custardy sweet base with a fluffy, foamy top. While this recipe does call for a raw egg yolk, according to local lore, the sodium bicarbonate and sodium citrate in the club soda supposedly "cooks" the yolk to reduce the chance of getting salmonella.

Makes 1 glass.

1 egg yolk
2 tablespoons sweetened condensed milk
6 ounces club soda, chilled

Add the egg yolk and sweetened condensed milk to a 12-ounce drinking glass. Whisk vigorously until smooth, then pour the club soda into the glass, continuing to whisk until well combined.

Note: This recipe uses a raw egg. Local lore aside, anyone pregnant, nursing, or with a compromised immune system should take care eating raw or undercooked eggs due to the risk of salmonella. I recommend using only your own cleanest, freshest eggs for this recipe or use pasteurized eggs.

Vietnamese Egg Coffee

(Cà Phê Trứng)

Growing up in a Scandinavian household in rural New England, I wasn't exposed to Asian cuisine until I started working in Manhattan after college. And I had never heard of Vietnamese Egg Coffee until I started writing cookbooks and doing a deep dive into unique ways to use eggs. But after one sip, I was hooked! This coffee is like liquid tiramisu in a glass. Thick, foamy, and sweet, it's everything a coffee should be. Unlike the quite utilitarian Swedish egg coffee (which I included in my first cookbook and which calls for crushing an entire egg, shell and all, into the coffee), Vietnamese Egg Coffee is more refined—and is pure indulgence. The recipe calls for a fair amount of espresso, but if that's too much caffeine for you, feel free to substitute with regular strong coffee.

Makes 2 cups.

4 egg yolks
2 tablespoons sweetened condensed milk
2 teaspoons sugar
1/2 teaspoon vanilla bean paste
6 ounces prepared espresso
Espresso powder or cocoa powder for dusting

With a hand mixer or in the bowl of a stand mixer fitted with the whisk attachment, beat the egg yolks, condensed milk, sugar, and vanilla bean paste on medium until combined. Increase the mixer speed to high and continue to beat for 5 minutes, until the mixture is thick and creamy and looks almost like a cake batter.

While the topping is whisking, divide the espresso into two heatproof drinking glasses or coffee mugs. Spoon the topping over the coffee, dividing it evenly between the two glasses. Dust with the espresso powder or cocoa powder and serve with a spoon. The coffee can be stirred to mix the topping into the liquid or simply sipped through the foamy topping.

Fresh Tip: To keep the espresso hot until the topping is ready, set the filled glasses in a shallow container of hot water.

Note: Consuming raw or undercooked eggs may increase your risk of foodborne illness, especially if you have certain medical conditions.

Honey Ginger Whiskey Sour

This riff on a classic whiskey sour calls for ginger-infused simple syrup for a bit of spice to complement the tart lemon juice. And the egg white foam on top makes for a beautiful presentation. The ginger needs time to steep in the syrup, so start that the night before, or keep some chilled in the fridge ready for your next happy hour. The simple syrup recipe can be doubled or tripled to make larger batches.

Makes 1 cocktail.

Ginger Simple Syrup

Makes about 3/4 cup.

1/2 cup water
2-inch piece ginger, peeled and thinly sliced
1/2 cup honey

Honey Ginger Whiskey Sour

1 ounce Ginger Simple Syrup
2 ounces whiskey
1 ounce freshly squeezed lemon juice, reserve a slice of lemon for garnish (about 1 lemon)
1 egg white, room temperature
Granulated sugar, for rimming the glass
Candied ginger, for garnish
Citrus bitters, for garnish
Lemon slice, for garnish

For the Simple Syrup

Combine the water and ginger in a small saucepan and bring to a boil. Reduce the heat and simmer for 5 minutes, then remove from the heat and stir or whisk in the honey. Let the liquid cool to room temperature, then strain out the ginger pieces, reserving one to rim the glass, and refrigerate until ready to use.

For the Cocktail

Rub the rim of a rocks or old-fashioned glass with the reserved piece of ginger, then press the rim into a plate of sugar.

Combine 1 ounce Ginger Simple Syrup, whiskey, lemon juice, and egg white in a cocktail shaker without ice. Dry shake vigorously for 30 seconds until the egg white is frothy. Add several ice cubes and shake for 20 seconds more to chill the ingredients. Strain into the prepared glass over ice. Dot a few drops of bitters on top and swirl with a toothpick. Garnish with a piece of candied ginger and a slice of lemon.

Fresh Tip: Store your fresh ginger in the freezer. Then it's easy to chop off pieces with a chef's knife and use the back of a spoon to remove the peel.

Note: Consuming raw or undercooked eggs may increase your risk of foodborne illness, especially if you have certain medical conditions.

Barista-Style Cinnamon Latte

If there's not a coffeehouse around the corner from where you live, why not become a barista on those chilly winter mornings when you have a little extra time or maybe are snowed in? This rich cinnamon coffee beverage is perfect for sipping in front of the fire while you work your way through a good book. The addition of the egg yolks adds an unexpected creaminess to each sip.

Makes 2 cups.

1 cup strong hot brewed coffee
1 cup whole milk
2 egg yolks
2 tablespoons granulated sugar
1 cinnamon stick
1/2 cup heavy cream, whipped to soft peaks
Ground cinnamon, for garnish
Swedish pearl sugar, for garnish

Divide the coffee into two large coffee mugs. In a medium saucepan over low heat, whisk the milk, egg yolks, and sugar until smooth, then add the cinnamon stick. Cook, stirring constantly for several minutes, until just warmed through and bubbles are just beginning to form around the edges, then remove from the heat. You don't want your mixture to boil, or it will curdle and break.

Remove the cinnamon stick, and top off the mugs with the hot milk mixture. Spoon a dollop of whipped cream on top, then garnish with ground cinnamon and pearl sugar.

Mulled Spiced Wine

(Scandinavian Glögg)

Glögg, or *gløgg*, is a spiced mulled wine that is sort of like a cross between sangria and cider. It's common throughout Scandinavia but especially in Sweden. With the warm notes of cinnamon, ginger, and cardamom, it's a nice way to end a day of skiing as you sit by the fire. Or enjoy a glass while you relax and watch a movie at home. It's also a nice big batch cocktail to make when you have guests. You can double or even triple the recipe. And you can use any red wine as your base, but I like a nice full-bodied Cabernet.

Makes 6 servings.

1 bottle red wine
1/2 cup granulated sugar
1 orange, sliced into 1/4-inch slices (reserve one slice per glass for garnish)
1 tablespoon whole green cardamom pods
1-inch piece fresh ginger, peeled and thinly sliced
2 cinnamon sticks, plus more for serving
4 or 5 star anise
Vanilla bean, split in half and the seeds scraped out
1/2 cup vodka

Add the red wine, sugar, orange slices, cardamom pods, ginger, cinnamon, star anise, vanilla bean, and vodka into a large pot or Dutch oven.

Heat over medium heat until bubbles start to form around the edges, stirring to dissolve the sugar. Reduce the heat to prevent the liquid from boiling so you don't boil off the alcohol. Continue to simmer for 2 to 3 minutes.

Remove the pot from the heat, cover, and let it stand for 10 to 15 minutes. Strain out the spices and orange slices, then pour the glögg into heatproof glass mugs.

Garnish each glass with a reserved orange slice and cinnamon stick and serve hot.

White Christmas Cocktail

Pillowy mounds of frothed egg white resemble snow in this festive holiday cocktail that's oh so good. The Sugared Cranberries and Rosemary need several hours to dry, and the simple syrup requires time to cool, so it's best to prepare both well in advance of serving this festive cocktail. The cocktail recipe itself is easily doubled (or quadrupled) for a crowd, and any extra simple syrup can be kept in the refrigerator for up to two weeks. The Sugared Cranberries and Rosemary can be refrigerated in an airtight container for up to four days.

Makes 1 cocktail.

Rosemary Simple Syrup
Makes about 1 1/2 cups.
1 cup water
1 cup granulated sugar
2 fresh rosemary sprigs

Sugared Cranberries and Rosemary
Makes enough for 4 cocktails.
1 egg white
2 tablespoons granulated sugar
4 fresh rosemary sprigs
12 fresh or frozen cranberries

White Christmas Cocktail
1 ounce chilled Rosemary Simple Syrup, plus more for dipping
1 teaspoon coarse sanding sugar
2 ounces chilled vodka
1 ounce chilled cranberry juice
1 teaspoon freshly squeezed lemon juice (less than 1/2 lemon)
1 egg white, room temperature
Sugared Cranberries and Rosemary, for garnish

For the Syrup
In a small saucepan over medium-high heat, stir or whisk the water and sugar. Bring to a simmer and continue to heat for several minutes, whisking or stirring occasionally to dissolve the sugar completely, then remove from the heat. Add the rosemary sprigs, steep for 15 minutes, then strain out the solids and pour the syrup into a glass jar. Cool to room temperature, then cover and refrigerate.

For the Cranberries and Rosemary
Line a small, rimmed baking sheet or square cake pan with parchment. In a small bowl whisk the egg white and 1 teaspoon water until foamy and well combined. Pour the sugar into a shallow dish. Dip the rosemary sprigs, one at a time, into the egg wash, shaking to remove any excess, then toss in the sugar. Shake to remove any excess sugar and place on the parchment-lined sheet pan to dry.

Repeat with the cranberries, dipping them first into the egg wash, then tossing them in sugar. Space them out on the parchment with the rosemary and let them dry completely at room temperature, at least 5 to 6 hours, preferably overnight.

Assemble the Cocktail
Pour some of the Rosemary Simple Syrup into a dish and dip the rim of a coupe glass into the syrup, then roll in the sugar. Add several ice cubes to the glass.

To a cocktail shaker or pint mason jar without ice, add the vodka, cranberry juice, lemon juice, 1 ounce simple syrup, and egg white. Dry shake vigorously until the egg white is foamed and very frothy, about 30 to 45 seconds. Add ice and shake again until chilled. Pour the liquid into the glass, adding more cranberry juice to top off if necessary, and garnish with the Sugared Cranberries and Rosemary.

Note: Consuming raw or undercooked eggs may increase your risk of foodborne illness, especially if you have certain medical conditions.

Seasonal Menus

Spring

Soups

Chilled Pea and Mint Soup
Milk and Egg Breakfast Soup
Shrimp Ball Egg Noodle Soup with Dill

Salads

Avocado, Goat Cheese, and Pecan Arugula Salad with Cherry Champagne Vinegar Dressing
Smoked Salmon Salad with Lemon and Dill
Strawberry Bacon Salad with Fried Halloumi and Creamy Honey Balsamic Dressing
Salmon Rice Bowls with Cucumber, Avocado, Frizzled Shallots, and Hot Honey Mayo

Sandwiches

Buttermilk Cheddar Biscuit Fried Egg Sliders with Honey Sage Browned Butter
Bacon, Egg, and Cheese Ciabatta Sandwiches with Maple Mayo
Smashed Eggs on Honey Ricotta Toast

Vegetables

Minted Peas with Goat Cheese and Honey
Fancy Honey-Roasted Carrots with Cardamom, Goat Cheese, and Ginger

Eggs

Maple Poached Eggs
Poached Eggs with Greek Avgolemono (Egg Lemon) Sauce
Poached Egg with Greek Yogurt, Fresh Herb Butter, and Honey
Quiche with Fresh Herbs and Cheese
Finnish Oven Pancake (Pannukakku) with Ricotta Honey Whip, Peas, and Asparagus
Asparagus, Cheddar, and Scallion Frittata
Creamy Baked Eggs with Parmesan, Black Olives, and Fresh Herbs
Smoked Gouda Egg Quesadilla with Baby Spinach
Avocado and Goat Cheese Breakfast Quesadillas
Green Goddess Deviled Eggs
Deep-Fried Deviled Eggs with Tarragon
Elegant Honeydew and Prosciutto-Rose Eggs

Berries and Fruit

Strawberry Cardamom Cream Cheese Crepes
One-Bowl Strawberry Scones with Almond Drizzle

Custard and Pudding

Warm Molten Lemon Soufflé Cakes
Lemon Butter Cookies with Lemon Curd Filling
Maple Brown Sugar Pots de Crème with Bourbon Whipped Cream

Cocktails and Beverages

Sydney Sunrise

Summer

Soups

Finnish Summer Soup (Kesäkeitto)
Chilled Watermelon Soup with Feta and Mint
Coconut Curry Shrimp Bowl with Jammy Eggs

Salads

Black and Bleu Berry Salad with Blueberry Balsamic Dressing
Creamy Scandinavian Cucumber Salad with Dill
Nectarine Panzanella Salad with Poached Eggs and Mint

Sandwiches

Peach Caprese Grilled Sandwiches with Fresh Mozzarella and Basil
Open-Faced Scandinavian Shrimp and Smoked Salmon Sandwiches (Smørrebrød)
Double-Decker Salmon Cake Sandwiches with Lemon Dill Mayo

Vegetables

Veggie Hash with Fresh Basil
Three-Cheese Tomato Tarts
Lemon-Butter-Bath Corn on the Cob with Hot Honey
Eggplant Parmesan Stacks with Basil Marinara

Eggs

Poached Eggs over Garlic Ginger Coconut Rice
Butter Beer–Poached Eggs
Bacon, Egg, and Cheese French Toast Bake
One-Pan Baked Creamy Eggs on Toast (Oeufs au Plat Bressanne)
French Omelets with Bleu Cheese and Chives
Fiesta Egg and Vegetable Quesadillas
Jammy Dressed Egg Flight
Caesar Deviled Eggs
Piña Colada Deviled Eggs

Berries and Fruit

Glazed Cardamom Peach Quick Bread
Grilled Apricot and Burrata Caprese with Honey and Herb Oil
Maine Wild Blueberry Pie
Mixed Berry Brown Sugar Crumble
Pretty in Pink Raspberry Party Cupcakes

Custard and Pudding

Honey Vanilla Yogurt Cups with Berries and Mint
Blackberry Basil Ice Cream

Cocktails and Beverages

Strawberry Basil Limeade
Blackberry Vanilla Shrub Cocktail
Vietnamese Egg Soda (Soda Sữa Hột Gà)
Vietnamese Egg Coffee (Cà Phê Trứng)

Fall

Soups

Creamy of Mushroom Soup with Sherry and Truffle Oil

Roasted Butternut Squash Soup with Fried Sage and Garlic Croutons

Salads

Potato Salad with Bacon, Eggs, and Fresh Herbs

Pickled Beet and Goat Cheese Salad with Pine Nuts and Raspberry Balsamic Dressing

Pear and Feta Salad with Tahini Miso Honey Dressing and Homemade Croutons

Wedge Salad with Bacon Fig Dressing

Sandwiches

Classic Croque Madame

Haddock Sandwiches with Cheddar Cheese and Lemon Garlic Aioli

Vegetables

Maple Bacon–Roasted Brussels Sprouts with Pistachios and Crispy Shallots

Mushrooms Sautéed in Sherry Garlic Butter and Thyme

Vanilla Parsnip Puree

Eggs

Steamed Eggs with Sweet Potato Puree

Finnish Oven Pancakes (Pannukakku) with Caramelized Onions, Walnuts, and Fontina

Egg and Mushroom Tart

Crunchy Baked Vanilla Bourbon French Toast Sticks

Mushroom Goat Cheese Omelets with Crispy Shallots and Sage

Cheesy Bacon and Egg Breakfast Tortillas

Garlic Oeufs Mayonnaise (Eggs with Mayo)

Black Forest Deviled Eggs

Berries and Fruit

Roasted Grapes with Walnuts, Feta, Rosemary, and Honey Balsamic Drizzle

Custard and Pudding

Pistachio Pudding

Earl Grey Crème Brûlée

Traditional New England Indian Pudding

Cocktails and Beverages

Honey Ginger Whiskey Sour

Winter

Soups

New England Seafood Chowder

Salads

Sesame Coleslaw
Citrus Avocado Salsa Salad

Sandwiches

Sriracha Mayo Fried Egg Sandwiches

Vegetables

Pub-Style Fries with Garlic Beer Aioli
Duchess Potatoes

Eggs

Norwegian Smoked Salmon Eggs Royale
Side Bar: Crispy Deep-Fried Poached Eggs
Monte Cristo Breakfast Bake
Mini Charcuterie Stratas
Cream Cheese and Lox Omelets with Capers and Dill
Eggs Jeanette
Smoked Salmon and Dill Holiday Deviled Eggs

Berries and Fruit

Creamed Rice with Cranberry Soup and Cardamom Whipped Cream (Riisipuuro)
Pink Grapefruit Brûlée with Tarragon Lime Sugar

Custard and Pudding

"Burnt" Basque Cheesecake
Deep-Dish French Silk Chocolate Hazelnut Pie
Portuguese Milk Tarts (Queijadas de Leite)

Cocktails and Beverages

Barista-Style Cinnamon Latte
Mulled Spiced Wine (Scandinavian Glögg)
White Christmas Cocktail

Acknowledgments

In my mind, this was to be a second egg cookbook, written as a follow-up to my first cookbook (*The Fresh Eggs Daily Cookbook*), because I have so many more delicious egg recipes I want to share with the world. But thanks to my agent and publisher who, in their infinite wisdom, requested that I expand my tunnel vision, this cookbook is the result (and thank goodness they did, considering the price of eggs these days!).

Because of them, this book is even more than I could ever have hoped for. So an immense thanks goes to the entire team who worked on *In Season*.

My agents at Park, Fine & Brower: John Maas, Sarah Passick, and Mia Vitale

The Harper Celebrate Team: Michael Aulisio, Danielle Peterson, Allison Picard, Sabryna Lugge, Robin Richardson, and Becky Tucker.

My publicists at The Brooks Group: Rebecca Brooks, Willie Norkin, Alyssa Braden, and Allie Santoro

A special thanks goes to all my readers who bought my first cookbook, paving the way for a second one.

And of course I need to thank my husband who, without complaint, eats the same thing over and over until I get the recipe just right, and the chickens who happily eat all the leftovers.

Speaking of chickens, I have to thank Vital Farms for generously providing all the eggs and butter for the photoshoot, since my own chickens were still on their annual strike at the time of the shoot—and we don't have a cow.

Index

C

F

G

M

N

O

About the Author

Lisa Steele is an author, popular television and radio personality, and creator of the blog *Fresh Eggs Daily*, the premier online resource for chicken-keeping advice. Lisa has amassed an audience of nearly one million from all over the globe, who look to her for tips on raising backyard poultry naturally, gardening tips, and her coop-to-kitchen recipes. Her previous books on chicken keeping have sold more than 150,000 copies worldwide and are among the bestselling chicken-keeping books in print. Her debut cookbook was an Amazon Editors' Pick for Best Cookbooks, Food & Wine.

Dubbed "queen of the coop" by the media, Lisa has been recognized by many national media outlets, including the *New York Times*, the *Wall Street Journal*, *Forbes*, *USA Today*, *Country Living*, *Farmers' Almanac*, *Real Simple*, *Southern Living*, *Martha.com*, and *Parade*. As a television and radio guest, Lisa has appeared on the Hallmark Channel's *Home & Family*, *Martha Knows Best* on HGTV, *P. Allen Smith's Garden Home*, and NPR's *Here & Now* and *Maine Calling*. Her first book was recommended summer reading on *The View* in 2018, and her website was featured on an episode of *The Dr. Oz Show* that was focused on eating eggs. Lisa also produced and hosted two seasons of the Telly Award–winning television show, *Welcome to My Farm*, on CreateTV/PBS.

A fifth-generation chicken keeper and Maine Master Gardener, Lisa lives in rural Maine with her husband, their corgi, and a mixed flock of almost two dozen hens, ducks, and geese.